DISCOVER DESKTOP CONFERENCING

The Directory Tab

Show properties

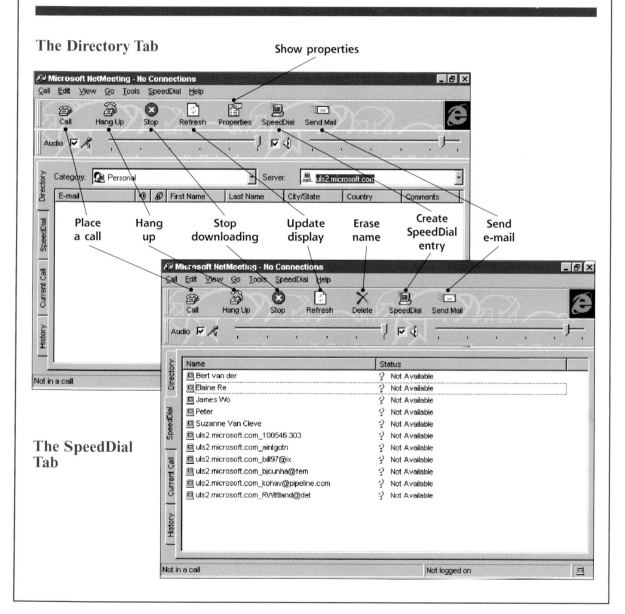

Place a call

Hang up

Stop downloading

Update display

Erase name

Create SpeedDial entry

Send e-mail

The SpeedDial Tab

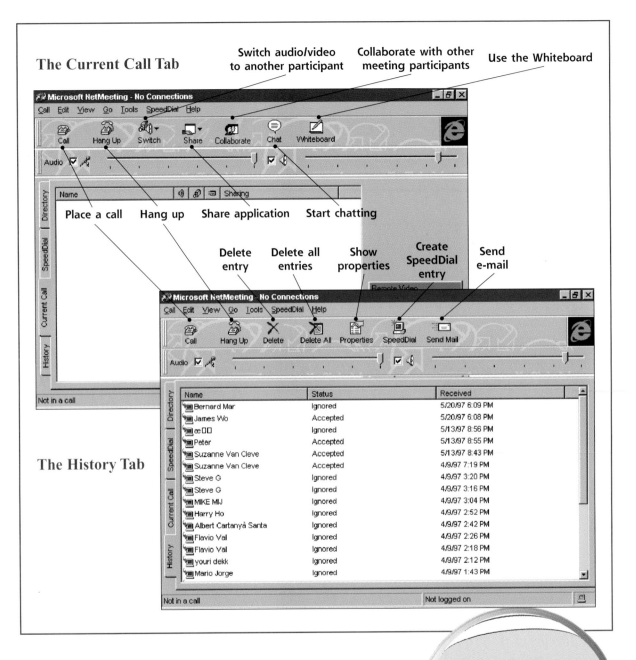

The Current Call Tab

Switch audio/video to another participant

Collaborate with other meeting participants

Use the Whiteboard

Place a call

Hang up

Share application

Start chatting

Delete entry

Delete all entries

Show properties

Create SpeedDial entry

Send e-mail

The History Tab

DISCOVERY CENTRAL

DISCOVER DESKTOP CONFERENCING WITH NETMEETING™ 2.0

DISCOVER DESKTOP CONFERENCING WITH NETMEETING™ 2.0

MIKE BRITTON AND
SUZANNE VAN CLEVE

IDG BOOKS WORLDWIDE, INC.

AN INTERNATIONAL
DATA GROUP COMPANY

FOSTER CITY, CA CHICAGO, IL
INDIANAPOLIS, IN SOUTHLAKE, TX

Discover Desktop Conferencing with NetMeeting ™ 2.0

Published by

IDG Books Worldwide, Inc.

An International Data Group Company
919 E. Hillsdale Blvd.
Suite 400
Foster City, CA 94404

www.idgbooks.com (IDG Books Worldwide Web site)

Library of Congress Catalog Card No.: 97-72188

ISBN: 0-7645-8037-X

Printed in the United States of America

10 9 8 7 6 5 4 3 2 1

1B/RU/QY/ZX/FC

Distributed in the United States by IDG Books Worldwide, Inc.

Distributed by Macmillan Canada for Canada; by Transworld Publishers Limited in the United Kingdom; by IDG Norge Books for Norway; by IDG Sweden Books for Sweden; by Woodslane Pty. Ltd. for Australia; by Woodslane Enterprises Ltd. for New Zealand; by Longman Singapore Publishers Ltd. for Singapore, Malaysia, Thailand, and Indonesia; by Simron Pty. Ltd. for South Africa; by Toppan Company Ltd. for Japan; by Distribuidora Cuspide for Argentina; by Livraria Cultura for Brazil; by Ediciencia S.A. for Ecuador; by Addison-Wesley Publishing Company for Korea; by Ediciones ZETA S.C.R. Ltda. for Peru; by WS Computer Publishing Corporation, Inc., for the Philippines; by Unalis Corporation for Taiwan; by Contemporanea de Ediciones for Venezuela; by Computer Book & Magazine Store for Puerto Rico; by Express Computer Distributors for the Caribbean and West Indies. Authorized Sales Agent: Anthony Rudkin Associates for the Middle East and North Africa.

For general information on IDG Books Worldwide's books in the U.S., please call our Consumer Customer Service department at 800-762-2974. For reseller information, including discounts and premium sales, please call our Reseller Customer Service department at 800-434-3422.

For information on where to purchase IDG Books Worldwide's books outside the U.S., please contact our International Sales department at 415-655-3200 or fax 415-655-3295.

For information on foreign language translations, please contact our Foreign & Subsidiary Rights department at 415-655-3021 or fax 415-655-3281.

For sales inquiries and special prices for bulk quantities, please contact our Sales department at 415-655-3200 or write to the address above.

For information on using IDG Books Worldwide's books in the classroom or for ordering examination copies, please contact our Educational Sales department at 800-434-2086 or fax 817-251-8174.

For press review copies, author interviews, or other publicity information, please contact our Public Relations department at 415-655-3000 or fax 415-655-3299.

For authorization to photocopy items for corporate, personal, or educational use, please contact Copyright Clearance Center, 222 Rosewood Drive, Danvers, MA 01923, or fax 508-750-4470.

is a trademark under exclusive license to IDG Books Worldwide, Inc., from International Data Group, Inc

ABOUT IDG BOOKS WORLDWIDE

Welcome to the world of IDG Books Worldwide.

IDG Books Worldwide, Inc., is a subsidiary of International Data Group, the world's largest publisher of computer-related information and the leading global provider of information services on information technology. IDG was founded more than 25 years ago and now employs more than 8,500 people worldwide. IDG publishes more than 275 computer publications in over 75 countries (see listing below). More than 60 million people read one or more IDG publications each month.

Launched in 1990, IDG Books Worldwide is today the #1 publisher of best-selling computer books in the United States. We are proud to have received eight awards from the Computer Press Association in recognition of editorial excellence and three from *Computer Currents'* First Annual Readers' Choice Awards. Our best-selling *...For Dummies*® series has more than 30 million copies in print with translations in 30 languages. IDG Books Worldwide, through a joint venture with IDG's Hi-Tech Beijing, became the first U.S. publisher to publish a computer book in the People's Republic of China. In record time, IDG Books Worldwide has become the first choice for millions of readers around the world who want to learn how to better manage their businesses.

Our mission is simple: Every one of our books is designed to bring extra value and skill-building instructions to the reader. Our books are written by experts who understand and care about our readers. The knowledge base of our editorial staff comes from years of experience in publishing, education, and journalism — experience we use to produce books for the '90s. In short, we care about books, so we attract the best people. We devote special attention to details such as audience, interior design, use of icons, and illustrations. And because we use an efficient process of authoring, editing, and desktop publishing our books electronically, we can spend more time ensuring superior content and spend less time on the technicalities of making books.

You can count on our commitment to deliver high-quality books at competitive prices on topics you want to read about. At IDG Books Worldwide, we continue in the IDG tradition of delivering quality for more than 25 years. You'll find no better book on a subject than one from IDG Books Worldwide.

John Kilcullen
John Kilcullen
CEO
IDG Books Worldwide, Inc.

Steven Berkowitz
Steven Berkowitz
President and Publisher
IDG Books Worldwide, Inc.

VIII
WINNER
Eighth Annual
Computer Press
Awards ≥1992

IX
WINNER
Ninth Annual
Computer Press
Awards ≥1993

X
WINNER
Tenth Annual
Computer Press
Awards ≥1994

XI
WINNER
Eleventh Annual
Computer Press
Awards ≥1995

IDG Books Worldwide, Inc., is a subsidiary of International Data Group, the world's largest publisher of computer-related information and the leading global provider of information services on information technology. International Data Group publishes over 275 computer publications in over 75 countries. Sixty million people read one or more International Data Group publications each month. International Data Group's publications include: ARGENTINA: Buyer's Guide, Computerworld Argentina, PC World Argentina; AUSTRALIA: Australian Macworld, Australian PC World, Australian Reseller News, Computerworld, IT Casebook, Network World, Publish, Webmaster; AUSTRIA: Computerwelt Osterreich, Networks Austria, PC Tip Austria; BANGLADESH: PC World Bangladesh; BELARUS: PC World Belarus; BELGIUM: Data News; BRAZIL: Annuário de Informática, Computerworld, Connections, Macworld, PC Player, PC World, Publish, Reseller News, Supergamepower; BULGARIA: Computerworld Bulgaria, Network World Bulgaria, PC & MacWorld Bulgaria; CANADA: CIO Canada, Client/Server World, ComputerWorld Canada, InfoWorld Canada, NetworkWorld Canada, WebWorld; CHILE: Computerworld Chile, PC World Chile; COLOMBIA: Computerworld Colombia, PC World Colombia; COSTA RICA: PC World Centro America; THE CZECH AND SLOVAK REPUBLICS: Computerworld Czechoslovakia, Macworld Czech Republic, PC World Czechoslovakia; DENMARK: Communications World Danmark, Computerworld Danmark, Macworld Danmark, PC World Danmark, Techworld Denmark; DOMINICAN REPUBLIC: PC World Republica Dominicana; ECUADOR: PC World Ecuador; EGYPT: Computerworld Middle East, PC World Middle East; EL SALVADOR: PC World Centro America; FINLAND: MikroPC, Tietoverkko, Tietoviikko; FRANCE: Distributique, Hebdo, Info PC, Le Monde Informatique, Macworld, Reseaux & Telecoms, WebMaster France; GERMANY: Computer Partner, Computerwoche, Computerwoche Extra, Computerwoche FOCUS, Global Online, Macwelt, PC Welt; GREECE: Amiga Computing, GamePro Greece, Multimedia World; GUATEMALA: PC World Centro America; HONDURAS: PC World Centro America; HONG KONG: Computerworld Hong Kong, PC World Hong Kong, Publish in Asia; HUNGARY: ABCD CD-ROM, Computerworld Szamitastechnika, Internetto online Magazine, PC World Hungary, PC-X Magazin Hungary; ICELAND: Tolvuheimur PC World Island; INDIA: Information Communications World, Information Systems Computerworld, PC World India, Publish in Asia; INDONESIA: InfoKomputer PC World, Komputek Computerworld, Publish in Asia; IRELAND: ComputerScope, PC Live!; ISRAEL: Macworld Israel, People & Computers/Computerworld; ITALY: Computerworld Italia, Macworld Italia, Networking Italia, PC World Italia; JAPAN: DTP World, Macworld Japan, Nikkei Personal Computing, OS/2 World Japan, SunWorld Japan, Windows NT World, Windows World Japan; KENYA: PC World East African; KOREA: Hi-Tech Information, Macworld Korea, PC World Korea; MACEDONIA: PC World Macedonia; MALAYSIA: Computerworld Malaysia, PC World Malaysia, Publish in Asia; MALTA: PC World Malta; MEXICO: Computerworld Mexico, PC World Mexico; MYANMAR: PC World Myanmar; NETHERLANDS: Computer! Totaal, LAN Internetworking Magazine, LAN World Buyers Guide, Macworld Netherlands, Net, WebWereld; NEW ZEALAND: Absolute Beginners Guide and Plain & Simple Series, Computer Buyer, Computer Industry Directory, Computerworld New Zealand, MTB, Network World, PC World New Zealand, PC World Centro America; NORWAY: Computerworld Norge, CW Rapport, Datamagasinet, Financial Rapport, Kursguide Norge, Macworld Norge, Multimediaworld Norge, PC World Ekspress Norge, PC World Nettverk, PC World Norge, PC World ProduktGuide Norge; PAKISTAN: Computerworld Pakistan; PANAMA: PC World Panama; PEOPLE'S REPUBLIC OF CHINA: China Computer Users, China Computerworld, China InfoWorld, China Telecom World Weekly, Computer & Communication, Electronic Design China, Electronics Today, Electronics Weekly, Game Software, PC World China, Popular Computer Week, Software Weekly, Software World, Telecom World; PERU: Computerworld Peru, PC World Profesional Peru, PC World SoHo Peru; PHILIPPINES: Click!, Computerworld Philippines, PC World Philippines, Publish in Asia; POLAND: Computerworld Poland, Computerworld Special Report Poland, Cyber, Macworld Poland, Networld Poland, PC World Komputer; PORTUGAL: Cerebro/PC World, Computerworld/Correio Informático, Dealer World Portugal, Mac*In/PC*In Portugal, Multimedia World; PUERTO RICO: PC World Puerto Rico; ROMANIA: Computerworld Romania, PC World Romania, Telecom Romania; RUSSIA: Computerworld Russia, Mir PK, Publish, Seti; SINGAPORE: Computerworld Singapore, PC World Singapore, Publish in Asia; SLOVENIA: Monitor; SOUTH AFRICA: Computing SA, Network World SA, Software World SA; SPAIN: Communicaciones World España, Computerworld España, Dealer World España, Macworld España, PC World España, SRI LANKA: Infolink PC World; SWEDEN: CAP&Design, Computer Sweden, Corporate Computing Sweden, Internetworld Sweden, it.branschen, MaxiData Sweden, MikroDatorn, Natverk & Kommunikation, PC World Sweden, PCaktiv, Windows World Sweden; SWITZERLAND: Computerworld Schweiz, Macworld Schweiz, PCtip; TAIWAN: Computerworld Taiwan, Macworld Taiwan, NEW ViSION/Publish, PC World Taiwan, Windows World Taiwan; THAILAND: Publish in Asia, Thai Computerworld; TURKEY: Computerworld Turkiye, Macworld Turkiye, Network World Turkiye, PC World Turkiye; UKRAINE: Computerworld Kiev, Multimedia World Ukraine, PC World Ukraine; UNITED KINGDOM: Acorn User UK, Amiga Action UK, Amiga Computing UK, Apple Talk UK, Computing, Macworld, Parents and Computers UK, PC Advisor, PC Home, PSX Pro, The WEB; UNITED STATES: Cable in the Classroom, CIO Magazine, Computerworld, DOS World, Federal Computer Week, GamePro Magazine, InfoWorld, I-Way, Macworld, Network World, PC Games, PC World, Publish, Video Event, THE WEB Magazine, and WebMaster; online webzines: JavaWorld, NetscapeWorld, and SunWorld Online; URUGUAY: InfoWorld Uruguay; VENEZUELA: Computerworld Venezuela, PC World Venezuela; and VIETNAM: PC World Vietnam. 3/24/97

Welcome to the Discover Series

Do you want to discover the best and most efficient ways to use your computer and learn about technology? Books in the Discover series teach you the essentials of technology with a friendly, confident approach. You'll find a Discover book on almost any subject — from the Internet to intranets, from Web design and programming to the business programs that make your life easier.

We've provided valuable, real-world examples that help you relate to topics faster. Discover books begin by introducing you to the main features of programs, so you start by doing something *immediately*. The focus is to teach you how to perform tasks that are useful and meaningful in your day-to-day work. You might create a document or graphic, explore your computer, surf the Web, or write a program. Whatever the task, you learn the most commonly used features, and focus on the best tips and techniques for doing your work. You'll get results quickly, and discover the best ways to use software and technology in your everyday life.

You may find the following elements and features in this book:

Discovery Central: This tearout card is a handy quick reference to important tasks or ideas covered in the book.

Quick Tour: The Quick Tour gets you started working with the book right away.

Real-Life Vignettes: Throughout the book you'll see one-page scenarios illustrating a real-life application of a topic covered.

Goals: Each chapter opens with a list of goals you can achieve by reading the chapter.

Side Trips: These asides include additional information about alternative or advanced ways to approach the topic covered.

Bonuses: Timesaving tips and more advanced techniques are covered in each chapter.

Discovery Center: This guide illustrates key procedures covered throughout the book.

Visual Index: You'll find real-world documents in the Visual Index, with page numbers pointing you to where you should turn to achieve the effects shown.

Throughout the book, you'll also notice some special icons and formatting:

 A Feature Focus icon highlights new features in the software's latest release, and points out significant differences between it and the previous version.

 Web Paths refer you to Web sites that provide additional information about the topic.

 Tips offer timesaving shortcuts, expert advice, quick techniques, or brief reminders.

 The X-Ref icon refers you to other chapters or sections for more information.

Pull Quotes emphasize important ideas that are covered in the chapter.

 Notes provide additional information or highlight special points of interest about a topic.

 The Caution icon alerts you to potential problems you should watch out for.

The Discover series delivers interesting, insightful, and inspiring information about technology to help you learn faster and retain more. So the next time you want to find answers to your technology questions, reach for a Discover book. We hope the entertaining, easy-to-read style puts you at ease and makes learning fun.

Credits

ACQUISITIONS EDITOR
John Osborn

DEVELOPMENT EDITORS
Ralph Moore
Stefan Grünwedel

COPY EDITORS
Judy Brunetti
Anne Friedman

TECHNICAL EDITOR
Stephen Pedrick

PROJECT COORDINATOR
Susan Parini

QUALITY CONTROL SPECIALIST
Mick Arellano

GRAPHICS AND PRODUCTION SPECIALISTS
Mario F. Amador
Dina F Quan
Mary Penn
Andreas F. Schueller
Mark Schumann

PROOFREADER
Mary Oby

INDEXER
Sherry Massey

BOOK DESIGN
Seventeenth Street Studios
Phyllis Beaty
Kurt Krames

About the Authors

Mike Britton and **Suzanne Van Cleve** are the principals of Van Cleve Britton Publishing, Ltd., providing authoring, editorial, design, and production services to publishers. They have co-authored *Discover Intranets* and revised the *Macworld PageMaker 6.5 Bible* and the *Macworld FreeHand 7 Bible* for IDG Books Worldwide. They have also developed computer book titles for Adobe Press and are contributors to Adobe.com. Together, they have over 30 years of expertise in the publishing industry, developing comprehensive information management and production systems for HarperCollins, Random House, Macmillan, Adobe Press, and Standard Publishing. Visit their site on the World Wide Web at http://www.vcbweb.com or e-mail them at suzannevan@earthlink.net.

PREFACE

Discover Desktop Conferencing with NetMeeting 2.0 is intended for anyone who wants to discover the world of desktop conferencing and use its capabilities to the fullest. It is designed to be a guidebook as well as a reference. You can sit back, read, and enjoy, or jump in and get your hands dirty right away.

If you are a manager, you'll discover how desktop conferencing can help you build a stronger organization. If you use the Internet for personal use, you'll learn how to find new friends and communicate with those you love.

Part One, "The Basics," introduces the basics of NetMeeting. You will become acquainted with the main features of the software and how to use them:

* Chapter 1, "A Tour of the Software," shows you how to start NetMeeting, view the main window, select commands from the menu, use the main toolbar, set the general preferences, and tour NetMeeting's features.

* Chapter 2, "The Internet Phone," introduces you to Internet telephony and covers tuning your audio, addressing a call, and making an Internet call.

* Chapter 3, "Application Sharing," teaches you all about sharing applications.

* Chapter 4, "File Transfers," discusses the basics of transferring files: setting file transfer preferences, transferring files to one or more participants, and receiving files.

* Chapter 5, "The Whiteboard," shows you how to use NetMeeting's most creative feature: adjusting the Whiteboard settings, using the Whiteboard features, and communicating on the Whiteboard.

* Chapter 6, "Chatting," covers NetMeeting's really fun part. You learn how to set Chat preferences and conduct a Chat session.

* Chapter 7, "Video Conferencing," is about the nuts and bolts of conducting desktop conferencing. It covers the hardware and physical requirements, setting the video preferences, and conducting a video conference session.

Part Two, "Collaborating with NetMeeting," shows you how to put the software into useful practice. You'll discover how NetMeeting can really work:

* Chapter 8, "User Location Service Directory," teaches you about the Microsoft User Location Server (ULS), which you can use in conjunction with NetMeeting to find other users with whom to conduct conferences. Besides covering setting ULS preferences, this chapter shows you how to update and customize the ULS directory.

* Chapter 9, "Virtual Meetings," discusses the pros and cons (and etiquette!) of virtual meetings, conducting a virtual meeting, and maximizing the virtual meeting experience.

* Chapter 10, "Customer Service and Technical Support," shows you how to provide virtual customer service and technical support to your customers or clients. Topics also include gathering and evaluating virtual data.

* Chapter 11, "Telecommuting," introduces you to this creative (and sometimes necessary) method of working outside of the regular business office. In addition to covering the pros and cons of telecommuting, this chapter shows you how to plan for telecommuting, buy the right hardware, and connect to an Internet Service Provider.

* Chapter 12, "Distance Learning," introduces the fascinating subject of learning from outside a regular classroom setting. You learn what technologies are being used for distance learning, as well as how to plan for distance learning and conduct an online learning course.

Part Three, "Benefits of NetMeeting," uncovers the benefits of desktop conferencing and shows you how to implement the technology in your business and personal life:

* Chapter 13, "Using NetMeeting in Your Personal Life," shows you how to make NetMeeting as useful after hours as it is during your workday. This chapter covers keeping in touch with friends and family, finding and making new acquaintances, searching for that special love, and using NetMeeting for entertainment and conducting research.

* Chapter 14, "Using NetMeeting in Your Business Life," summarizes just how useful NetMeeting can be for your business. You'll learn that NetMeeting reduces travel costs, provides instant access to people and information, allows you to provide better customer service, and reduces the cost of storing information.

Finally, the back of the book contains several appendixes that cover finding, downloading, and installing NetMeeting 2.0 or Microsoft Chat 2.0 from the book's CD-ROM or the Internet, as well as what the requirements are for configuring NetMeeting or Chat on your system. There's also a list of frequently asked questions (FAQs) specific to using NetMeeting.

CONTENTS AT A GLANCE

PART THREE—BENEFITS OF NETMEETING

CONTENTS

VIRTUAL MEETING QUICK TOUR

To demonstrate what a virtual meeting would be like and what you need to do to conduct a virtual meeting, here's a quick trip into the world of virtual meetings.

Virtual meetings can dramatically change how people perceive meetings in your organization, but be forewarned: Reactions are bound to be mixed. Virtual meetings can be a terrific time and expense saver, because your attendees simply have to get to the computer or conference room nearby to join the meeting (Figure 1). These meetings are also new and very scary to some people who may have a hard time getting their ideas heard when they have to break through the technical barriers as well as social ones. Many people are shy about public speaking.

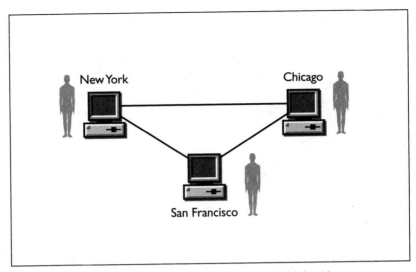

Figure 1 Virtual meetings can link participants in multiple cities.

In a virtual meeting, you can connect other participants at any time, and you can share comments from an unlimited number of people through the Chat feature. You can show what you're talking about with the Whiteboard, and you can communicate even more effectively when your voice is complimented with video.

As the meeting manager, you must instill the importance of the meeting in your attendees, and make it clear that it's the new way of operations. You can and should still have fun with video and the Whiteboard, but watch for people with hidden agendas who may attempt to limit the effectiveness of your virtual meeting.

Consider the following items when you organize a virtual meeting:

* **Who #1:** Who is going to lead the meeting?
* **Who #2:** Who is going to participate?
* **What:** What is the meeting for, anyway?
* **Where:** Where will each participant be located? You'll need to make sure that NetMeeting is properly installed and configured at each location.
* **When:** Pick a time that's convenient for everyone.
* **Why:** Set tangible goals for your meeting so everyone knows what they'll get for their time.
* **How:** Decide what virtual conferencing tools you will use.

Conducting a Virtual Meeting

N ow you're ready to conduct your first virtual meeting. Remember that it's a new experience for everyone, so lay the ground rules and encourage participants to follow them.

Connect the Participants

The first step in a virtual meeting is to connect all the participants and make sure that everyone can communicate. Otherwise, your meeting will not accomplish its intended purpose.

To begin your first virtual meeting, follow these steps:

1. Select **Programs** from the Windows 95 **Start** menu and locate NetMeeting. Click it to launch the application. (If this is your first time using NetMeeting, see Chapter 1 for information on the initial configuration for the program.)

2. If you're not already connected to your ISP, connect now. You will also automatically log on to a ULS directory when you connect.

3. Select the name of the person you want to call from the directory window, and then click the Call icon in the main toolbar.

4. An incoming dialog box (Figure 2) appears on the computer of the person you are trying to call. To answer your call, the person you are calling will click Accept.

Figure 2   The person you are calling sees this dialog when their phone "rings."

5. When the call is accepted, the Current Call window (Figure 3) will list you and the person who accepted your call.

6. To connect other participants, repeat Steps 3 and 4 until everyone who is supposed to be in the meeting is listed. As others enter the conference, their names will be listed in the Current Call window as well (Figure 3).

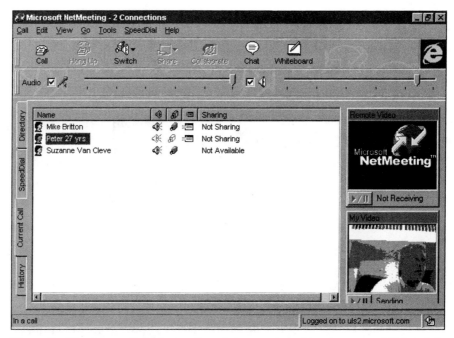

Figure 3 The Current Call window lists all the names and hardware capabilities of the meeting participants.

Introduce the Participants

It's easy to introduce the participants, whether you're using a video conference or not. Remember that only the first two people in the conference have audio and video capabilities. If it's a large meeting, you can introduce people via the Chat feature by listing participants and some background on why they're participating (their department, divisions, job title, and so on).

Chat is the tool you will use most in a multiperson conference because only the first two participants have audio or video capabilities.

Review the Agenda, Goals, and Time Frame

To immediately focus your meeting, display the agenda for everyone through the Chat feature and ask them to review it. Again, prepare and save the agenda ahead of time. Make sure everyone is aware of time frames, for each segment and for the end of the meeting.

File Transferring During the Meeting

Transferring files is a great asset, especially when someone arrives to your meeting without the necessary reports or documents (see Figure 4). Gone are the days of frantically trying to find fax machines located close to both the sender and recipient. You can send a file to all or any specific participant.

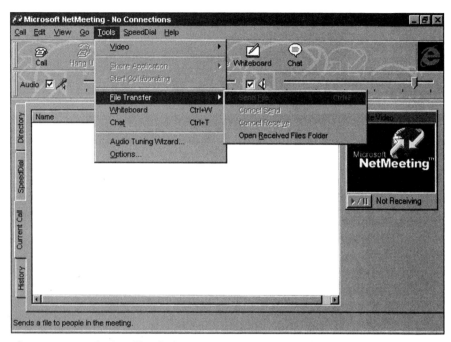

Figure 4 Transferring files during a meeting is simple using the menu command.

 ## Application Sharing During the Meeting

Sharing applications during a meeting is useful for viewing and discussing documents created in applications that all participants may not have. For example, suppose you want to show a slide presentation created in Persuasion, a book cover created in QuarkXPress, or a spreadsheet created in Lotus 1-2-3. Your participants only have the Microsoft Office suite and can't open any of these files themselves. Simply share the application in which you created the document and everyone can view your file.

 ## Drawing During the Meeting

The Whiteboard feature (see Figure 5) is a handy tool for everyone to sketch their ideas, just like an old-fashioned meeting with flipcharts. The best part is that everyone immediately has a copy to keep, print, file, or edit at will.

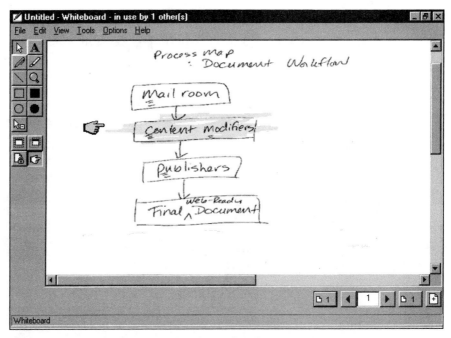

Figure 5 Using the Whiteboard to draw a flowchart.

You can copy and paste a chart onto the Whiteboard and use the Highlight tool and/or Remote Pointer. With the Whiteboard feature, you can copy and paste a spreadsheet to review budgets, a picture to discuss artwork, a contract to review, and so forth.

Wrapping Up the Meeting

When you're nearing the close of the meeting, take a few minutes to review the session and make sure everyone agrees on what transpired.

Disconnecting the Participants

After you have successfully conducted your virtual meeting, it's time to say goodbye and make sure that everyone is disconnected.

To disconnect from NetMeeting, follow these steps:

1. Notify the participants in the conference that you are hanging up, and then click Hang Up from the main toolbar.

2. To exit the program, choose Call → Exit from the menu bar.

PART ONE

THE BASICS

THIS PART CONTAINS THE FOLLOWING CHAPTERS

Welcome to video conferencing with NetMeeting. In Part One, you discover everything there is to know about the NetMeeting software and how to use NetMeeting's major features. Have you ever wanted to talk to your family and friends for as long as you like and not incur expensive phone bills? Visit Chapter 2 and discover the joys and wonders of the Internet Phone. Not only can you talk on the Internet, but you can augment your phone conversations, be they for business or for pleasure, by sharing documents, photos, drawings, and even live video of yourself. The future is now with NetMeeting, and Part One details each of these amazing features and more to get you going full speed ahead.

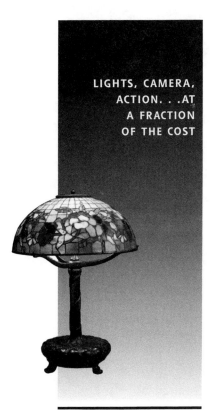

For TechnoMedia, a large media company specializing in book publishing, desktop video conferencing has reinvented their corporate-conferencing strategy. With over 4,000 employees in eight North American locations, conducting corporate-wide meetings can be a nightmare. Five years ago, Tom, the manager in charge of internal communications, purchased a proprietary video conferencing system to reduce the travel time and costs associated with their monthly managers' meetings.The system was expensive to operate and required a dedicated staff in each location to set up and monitor their conferences each time they conducted a meeting. "It usually took longer to set up the video and audio connections than actually run the meeting," laments Tom. Even worse, he says, was the embarrassment of fiddling with obtuse technology in front of the top executives gathered for an important meeting. Add to all that frustration a $200 per-hour rate for connect time, and Tom was thinking about job jeopardy!

Well, no more. Tom recently convinced his company to pilot a desktop video conferencing program. Monthy meetings use Microsoft NetMeeting and a Connectix QuickCam right on each participant's personal computer. Team members log on to the Internet, launch NetMeeting, and use the Audio Conferencing and Chat features the most. The Whiteboard comes into play for making points, and team members can transfer files during the session. The meetings are usually more productive, shorter, and to the point because the conference takes place at the team member's desk. People do miss spending several minutes before and after each meeting talking about personal issues and discussing how many meetings they must attend, but nobody's complaining. As Tom points out, "Most people are thrilled that they won't have to travel as frequently anymore. That gets real old after awhile."

Tom now receives accolades for an effective and smart system, and he estimates that the cost savings for eliminating the proprietary system will pay for the new cameras and software within a year. But Tom's greatest reward is a recent request to install a similar system soon for the Corporate Executive Committee. So, in effect, NetMeeting took a potentially embarrassing situation and turned it around completely.

A TOUR OF THE SOFTWARE

IN THIS CHAPTER YOU LEARN THESE KEY SKILLS

When you move to a new city, it's always a good idea to take a tour of the neighborhood. You need to locate the best grocery store and the closest bank. You need to understand how the community works so that you can make the most of your new home. Moving to a new piece of software is much like moving to a new city. You need to locate the functions in the software and learn the easiest way to accomplish a task. By doing this, you will make the most of your new software. NetMeeting is a revolutionary and evolutionary new way to improve the effectiveness by which two or more people interact. In the case of NetMeeting, you not only need to learn a new software program, you also need to learn a new way of communicating. This chapter is designed to familiarize you with the NetMeeting software. You'll take a tour around the menu options, learn how to use the toolbar, set preferences, and understand all the features of NetMeeting. This chapter is meant to be an introduction and an overview. If you are an accomplished Windows user, skim through the overview of the features and proceed onto Chapter 2. If you are just beginning, this chapter is the place to start.

✏ NOTE For a preview of a few of the important features you'll find in this chapter, turn to the Discovery Center. You can use the page references in the Discovery Center to quickly find additional information about each feature.

Starting NetMeeting

A s with any software, the first step in using the program is to find and launch the application (see Appendix A for installation instructions). Depending on where you installed the program and your level of expertise in Windows, this could be very easy or somewhat difficult.

To find NetMeeting, follow these steps:

1. Click the Start button. You see the Start menu options.

2. Click [**Programs**]. You see the programs and the program folders you have set up on your system.

3. Locate Microsoft NetMeeting in the list of programs and folders. If you have installed NetMeeting in the Programs folder, not in a subdirectory, you should see something like Figure 1-1.

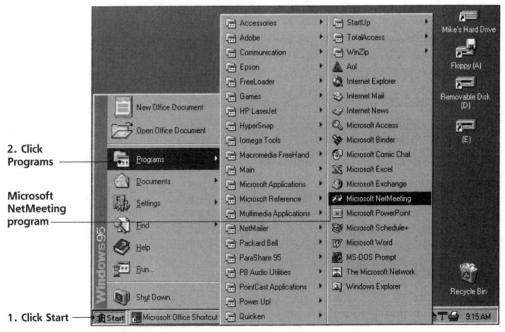

Figure 1-1 Finding NetMeeting using the Start menu.

To launch the software itself, you should follow these steps:

1. Click the NetMeeting icon.

2. The NetMeeting splash screen appears, as shown in Figure 1-2.

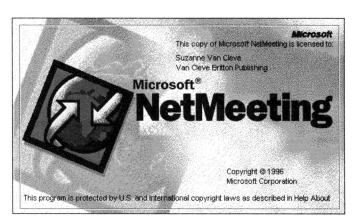

Figure 1-2 The NetMeeting splash screen.

3. If you are not already connected to your Internet Service Provider, the Dial-Up Networking dialog box (similar to the one shown in Figure 1-3) will appear. Make sure that each field contains the correct and appropriate information for your account and click Connect. If you are already connected to your ISP when you launch NetMeeting, this dialog box will not appear.

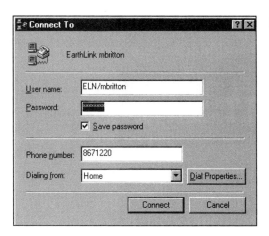

Figure 1-3 The Microsoft Dial-Up Connection window.

4. If you successfully connect, you're in business and can proceed to the next section to configure NetMeeting.

If you do not successfully connect to your service provider, you will see the dialog box shown in Figure 1-4. Click OK and NetMeeting will launch, but you will have no connection. Proceed to Step 5.

Figure 1-4 Your NetMeeting connection has failed.

5. Choose the `File` → `Exit` command to exit NetMeeting.

6. Check your connection information, and then go to Step 1 and retry. If problems still persist, call your Internet Service Provider for help.

Configuring the Software

The first time you launch NetMeeting, a setup wizard appears and prompts you for some personal information and the name of the User Location Server (ULS) you want to use (you can learn more about the purposes of the ULS in Chapter 8). Simply follow the instructions and answer your friendly wizard and in no time you will be looking at the NetMeeting main window. The wizard will not appear each time you run the software, only on the initial launch.

To configure the software, follow these steps:

1. Complete the steps in the two previous sections to find and launch the software. When the wizard appears, proceed to the next step.

2. Click Next.

3. Enter the appropriate personal information. Note that although the City/State, Country, and Comments fields are optional, it's better to fill in these boxes as well.

4. Click Next.

5. Check Yes if you want your name to be included on a ULS directory, or check No if you do not want your name listed (see Figure 1-5). You do have the choice, but at this time it's better to check Yes and have your name listed.

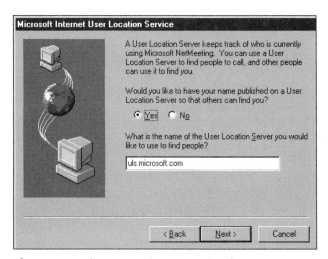

Figure 1-5 The NetMeeting Setup wizard.

6. For now, use the default ULS server displayed in the option box. You can always change any setup information at anytime. (You will be able to make a better decision as to what's right for you after reading the first eight chapters of this book.)

7. Click Next.

8. The Audio Tuning Wizard appears if you have a sound card in your computer. If you do not have a sound card, go to Step 10.

9. Follow the instructions for tuning your microphone, or read detailed instructions in Chapter 2.

10. Click Finish.

11. Your initial configuration of NetMeeting is now complete. (For more information on NetMeeting configuration, see Appendix B.)

Viewing the Main Window

When you launch NetMeeting successfully, you will see the main window, as shown in Figure 1-6. You might think of it as the master control center for the program. Every feature of NetMeeting is accessed from this area. You must understand all the features in this window to use the software effectively. This section helps you do just that.

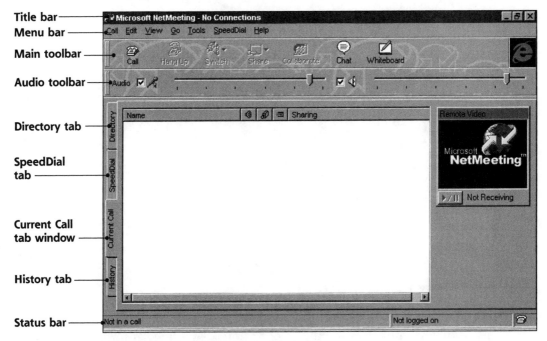

Figure 1-6 The NetMeeting main window.

The main window contains the following elements:

* Title bar
* Menu bar
* Main toolbar
* Audio toolbar
* Directory tab window
* SpeedDial tab window

* Current Call tab window
* History tab window
* Status bar

Title Bar

The title bar shows the program name and the name of your NetMeeting connection, if any. It also contains the Windows minimize, maximize, and close buttons, as well as the Windows menu.

Menu Bar

The menu bar lists the menu names for the application. From this area, you can access all of NetMeeting's functionality. (See the later section "Selecting Commands from the Menu" for more information.)

Main Toolbar

The toolbar is a graphical representation of frequently used commands from the menu and is designed to save time. You can click the appropriate button to select a command instead of accessing the command from the menu bar. For instance, to launch the Whiteboard feature, click the Whiteboard button. (See the section "Using the Main Toolbar" for more information.) The main toolbar changes as you select the different tab windows.

Audio Toolbar

The audio toolbar allows you to adjust microphone and speaker settings. The check boxes toggle on and off to mute your voice and turn off your speakers.

 See the section "Audio Tuning" in Chapter 2 for more details.

Directory Tab Window

The Directory tab window lists the NetMeeting users who are currently on the network and available for contact. E-mail address, First Name, Last Name, City/State, Country, and Comments are the fields in this window. You can also see whether each NetMeeting user has audio and video capabilities in the speaker and camera columns, as shown in Figure 1-7. (See the section "Making an Internet Call" in Chapter 2 for more information.)

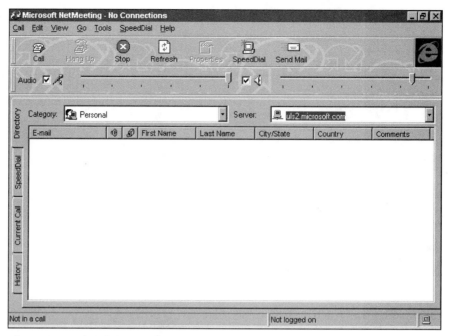

Figure 1-7 The Directory tab window.

SpeedDial Tab Window

The SpeedDial tab window shows your current list of NetMeeting friends and family that you can contact with just a click. This feature works much like the speed dial feature on most telephones. You can see the name and status of everyone in your SpeedDial directory (see Figure 1-8).

Current Call Tab Window

The Current Call tab window shows your current NetMeeting connections. In a multiple-person conference, this is very valuable information. (See Chapter 2 for more information.) If there are no connections, the Current Call tab window looks like Figure 1-9.

History Tab Window

The History tab window is a log of your NetMeeting activity. From this window, you can see everyone that you have tried to contact and those who have called you (see Figure 1-10).

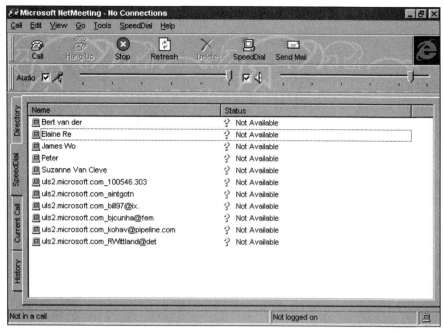

Figure 1-8 The SpeedDial tab window.

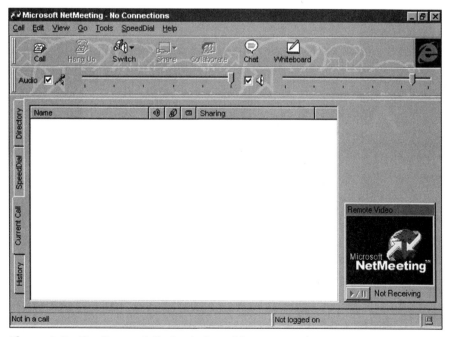

Figure 1-9 The Current Call tab window with no connections.

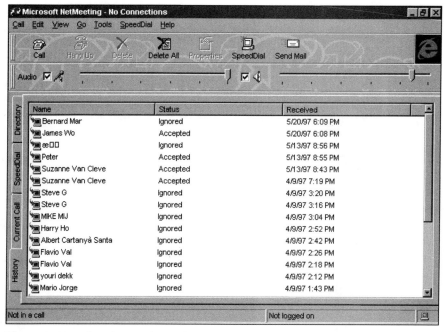

Figure 1-10 The History tab window.

Status Bar

The status bar shows your current connection status. You can find this information in other areas of the NetMeeting window as well. (See Chapter 2 for more information.)

TIP Microsoft allows you to access commands and view information, such as connection status, in a variety of ways. Sometimes this assortment can be very confusing. To minimize the amount of data your brain needs to keep in its RAM, determine the easiest way for you to accomplish a task or view information and consistently use that method. Even though Microsoft has provided all the bells and whistles, you don't have to use them.

Selecting Commands from the Menu

The heart of any Windows program is the menu bar. From this location, you can access all the program commands. Fortunately, NetMeeting's menu bar is rather simple to understand and use, as shown in Figure 1-11. The menu choices are as follows:

* Call
* Edit
* View
* Go
* Tools
* SpeedDial
* Help

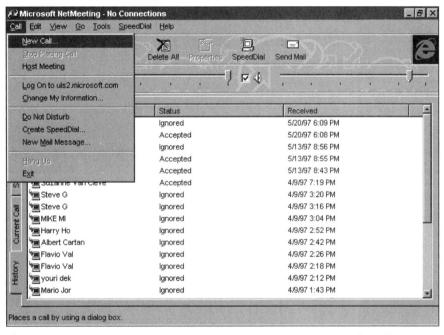

Figure 1-11   The NetMeeting menu bar showing the commands in the Call menu.

Touring the Menu Bar

The menu bar contains seven menu items — Call, Edit, View, Go, Tools, SpeedDial, and Help. Each of these contains the commands that make NetMeeting work. Table 1-1 shows the complete list of commands and key commands if available. Use this table as a reference and don't be concerned if you don't understand what the commands do. Each command is explained at the appropriate time throughout the book.

TABLE 1-1   Menu Bar Commands

Menu	Commands	Key Command
Call	New Call	
	Stop Placing Call	
	Host Meeting	
	Log Off from … (*ALTERNATE*: Log On to …)	
	Change My Information	
	Do Not Disturb	
	Create SpeedDial	
	New Mail Message	
	Hang Up	
	Exit	
Edit	Cut	Ctrl+X
	Copy	Ctrl+C
	Paste	Ctrl+V
View	Toolbar	
	Status Bar	
	Directory	
	SpeedDial	
	Current Call	
	History	
	Detach My Video	
	Detach Remote Video	
	Stop	
	Refresh	F5
Go	Web Directory	
	Home Page	
	Search the Web	
	Best of the Web	

Menu	Commands	Key Command
	Mail	
	News	
Tools	Switch Audio and Video	
	Video	
	Share Application	
	Start Collaborating	
	Chat	Ctrl+T
	Whiteboard	Ctrl+W
	File Transfer	
	Audio Tuning Wizard	
	Options	
SpeedDial	Add SpeedDial	
Help	Help Topics	
	Read Me	
	Microsoft on the Web	
	Online Support	
	About Microsoft NetMeeting	

How to Select a Command from the Menu Bar

Selecting a command in NetMeeting is exactly the same as any other Windows application. If this is old hat, just skip this section. If you're not quite sure how to do it, read on.

To select a command for the menu bar, follow these steps.

1. Click the menu item you want to access. For this example, choose the **Tools** menu.

2. Choose the **Whiteboard** Whiteboard command and the Whiteboard appears. It's that simple.

TIP Using a key command eliminates time-consuming mouse movements and offers a way to access menu commands without your fingers leaving the keyboard. To access the Whiteboard using a key command, simply press Ctrl+W and the Whiteboard appears just like it did in the previous example, but in half the time.

Using the Main Toolbar

The main toolbar is a graphical representation of the most popular menu commands. By clicking an icon, you access that command. When you move the cursor on top of an icon, it becomes a 3-D button and changes color. This indicates the command is live and ready for use. If the icon looks like it has a gray outline, the command is not currently a *live* option, which means that it is not available in your current situation (for example, if you are not currently in a call, the Hang Up button would be grayed out because you have nothing from which to hang up). The main toolbar contains icons that change to represent the tool options in each particular tab.

Setting General Preferences

NetMeeting is designed to allow you to customize the software to suit your individual needs and desires. Some customizations are technical in nature (such as the protocol preferences), and some are very personal (such as the Directory preferences, where you can divulge personal data about yourself). All these preferences are discussed in later chapters. NetMeeting's General preferences window contains some options that should be configured as part of your initial tour of the software; then you might just wonder why others are there in the first place. The next section helps you sort out this issue.

Finding the General Preferences

To access the general preferences for NetMeeting, choose Tools → Options from the menu bar. The NetMeeting Options window appears, as shown in Figure 1-12. This window contains six tabbed sections with the General preferences window displayed as the default.

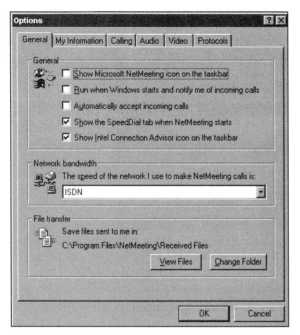

Figure 1-12 The General preferences window.

Understanding the Options

The General preferences window offers you seven options divided into three categories. To assign your preferences, you either check a check box, or choose a file from a pop-up window.

Choosing the Right Options

As you have probably figured out by now, some of the general options are pretty self-explanatory and several, such as offering you the choice of seeing the NetMeeting icon in the taskbar, aren't very useful. However, the *Run when Windows starts and notify me of incoming calls* option should be chosen to maximize the use of your software; all the other preferences are optional.

Touring NetMeeting's Features

The NetMeeting program is a combination of several different communication methods. Voice, video, data, pictures, sounds, and text make up the NetMeeting product. In this section, you learn how NetMeeting uses these communication methods by exploring the eight major features of the software, each of which is discussed in greater detail in subsequent chapters of this book:

* Internet Phone
* Application Sharing
* Shared Clipboard
* File Transfers
* The Whiteboard
* Chatting
* Video Conference
* The User Location Service Directory

The Internet Phone

One of the most exciting features of NetMeeting is Internet Phone. You can place a voice call to an associate over your intranet, call a friend across the country over the Internet, or make a new acquaintance on the far side of the globe without paying any additional phone charges. The Internet Phone feature uses a range of compression formats that optimize the audio signal for the speed of your network or modem connection. Figure 1-13 shows the Internet Phone feature.

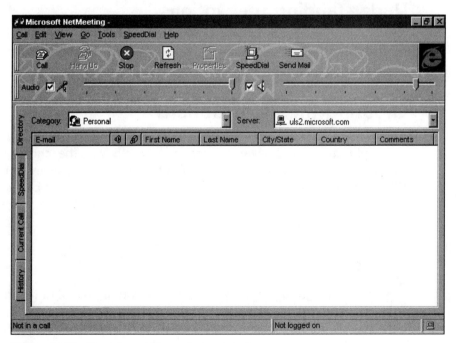

Figure 1-13 The Internet Phone feature window.

Application Sharing

The Application Sharing feature allows you to share a program (such as the Calculator program shown in Figure 1-14) running on your computer with other people in the NetMeeting conference. They will see the same information that you see on your computer. To take this one step further, you can choose to collaborate with your conference attendees, giving them the opportunity to edit and control the application. The fantastic thing about Application Sharing is that conference attendees do not need to have the application you're running, in order to participate. They can see, edit, and control the program as if they had the software. This ability opens the door for some very creative ways to use NetMeeting, as you will see throughout this book.

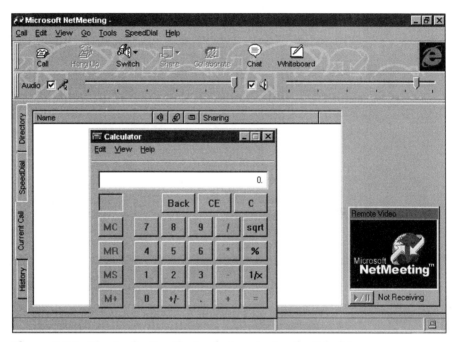

Figure 1-14   The Application Sharing feature sharing the Calculator program.

Shared Clipboard

The Shared Clipboard feature goes hand-in-hand with the previous section on Application Sharing. You can share the contents of your clipboard with other participants in a conference. You can copy information from any document and paste it into a shared application by using the familiar cut/copy/paste operation, as shown in Figure 1-15.

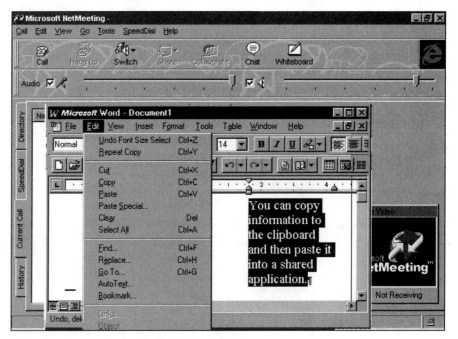

Figure 1-15 Using the Shared Clipboard feature.

File Transfers

With the File Transfer feature, you can send a file to the person you are con-nected to in NetMeeting, or to a group of people if you are in a conference. You can send any file saved on your computer, as shown in Figure 1-16. The file transfer happens in the background so you can continue to participate in the conference while your file zooms its way to the intended recipients.

The Whiteboard

The Whiteboard is probably the most amusing feature in NetMeeting. It is a multipage, multiuser drawing application that allows you to sketch diagrams and display graphical information to others in your NetMeeting conference. Figure 1-17 shows the Whiteboard feature. There are many uses for the Whiteboard and it's just plain fun. Whether you are an accomplished artist or a person who has a hard time drawing a line, the Whiteboard is sure to put a smile on your face.

 For more detailed information about the Whiteboard, see Chapter 5.

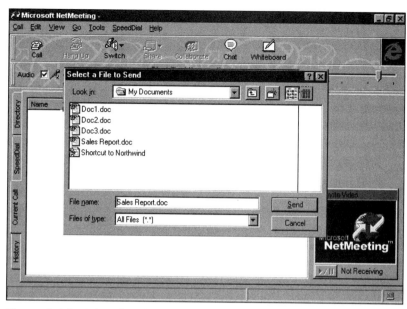

Figure 1-16   Using the File Transfer feature.

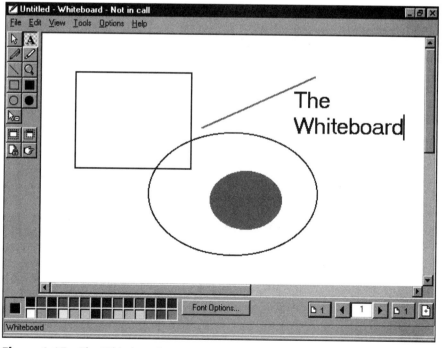

Figure 1-17   The Whiteboard.

Chatting

The Chat feature provides a text-based method of communication with one or more people. This feature is a handy thing to have because not everyone has the hardware to send and receive audio transmissions. The Chat window, shown in Figure 1-18, functions like other chat applications but can be used in combination with other NetMeeting features.

 X-REF   For more information on Chat, see Chapter 6.)

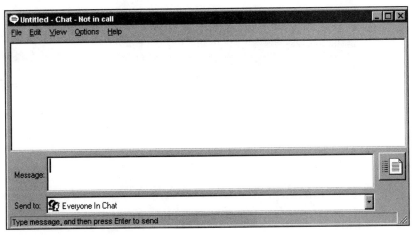

Figure 1-18   The Chat window.

Video Conferencing

This exciting feature is new to NetMeeting 2.0. Video Conferencing allows you to send and receive live video communications. You can receive video messages even if you don't have a video camera connected to your computer. Figure 1-19 shows the Video Conferencing window.

X-REF   For details on this feature, see Chapter 7.

Figure 1-19 Using the Video Conferencing feature.

The User Location Service Directory

With the User Location Service directory, you can find other NetMeeting users to talk to. The User Location Server (ULS) is a dynamic phone book. Users currently running NetMeeting are accessible directly from within NetMeeting or from a Web page. Microsoft has established a network of ULS servers, as shown in Figure 1-20, and third parties can implement their own ULS servers.

X-REF For more information on the User Location Service directory, see Chapter 8.

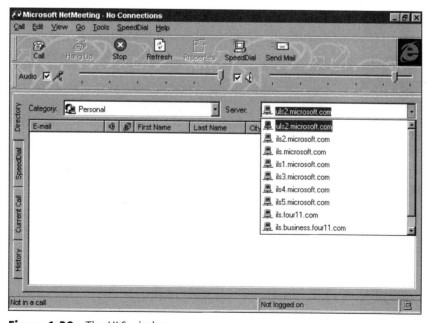

Figure 1-20 The ULS window.

BONUS

Maximizing Your Performance

NetMeeting allows you to connect to people in a variety of ways. You can use a local area network (LAN) by using the TCP/IP or IPX/SPX protocol. You can access a person over the Internet through an Internet Service Provider by using the TCP/IP protocol. You can also use a standard telephone line with a modem and make a direct connection (computer to computer). By making the right choices, you can maximize the performance of your computer. It all depends on your hardware, network, and your needs. This book provides detailed information on the technical side of maximizing your computer's performance in Appendix B. In addition to the technical aspect of performance, there is a nontechnical aspect of maximizing performance. This nontechnical aspect has to do with the time and effort you give to understanding the software that you use, and eliminating the extraneous pieces you don't need.

This chapter has explained the menus, buttons, and features of NetMeeting. By no means is it the most exciting chapter in the book — it's not even close! However, it could be one of the most important chapters because it lays a foundation on which to apply the software. Understanding up-front how the software thinks and behaves will save you countless hours of head-scratching and mouse-throwing. This applies to any software package that you use. The tendency is to jump into Chapter 14 — you know, the fun chapter — and never read the instructions. That might be more pleasurable in the short run, but not profitable for the long term. Maximize your performance by starting at the beginning and build a knowledge base of the application.

You may be saying to yourself, "That's okay for a program like NetMeeting; it doesn't have thousands of features. But what about a program like Microsoft Word? There's no way to start at the beginning and work your way through that." If that's what you think, you'd be absolutely correct. Unless you have a brain the size of Kansas, it's impossible to retain all that information. Software manufacturers have made their programs so big that it's impossible to understand all the features. The good news is you don't need to understand all the features, only the ones that apply to your particular application. The bad news is that most documentation from the software company isn't application-oriented. But there is more good news: Books like this one guide you past the extraneous information and bring you to the heart of the matter. This book has as much to do with how you apply NetMeeting as it does with how to use NetMeeting.

As you look at the inventory of software on your hard drive, ask yourself these questions: How many programs do you really understand? How many applications have you maximized for performance by eliminating the things you don't need? How many programs do you really apply? Read Appendix B to maximize your hardware; read the rest of this book to maximize your software.

Summary

This chapter covered some of the basics of the NetMeeting interface. You learned about the primary ways of accessing a command in NetMeeting — the menu bar and the main toolbar. You also learned the key commands for several of these operations.

You explored the general preferences of NetMeeting and learned what options to select. You then took a tour of the software to understand the eight main features of NetMeeting. This provided you the basic information you need to explore the full capabilities of the software in the remaining chapters of this book.

If you feel confident with the NetMeeting interface and features, it's time to proceed onto the meat of the book. If you still have some reservations, re-read this chapter. Over the next few pages, you learn how to properly use the software. From there, you explore how to apply the software to communicate in virtual meetings, customer service, technical support, telecommuting, and distance learning. After you understand how to use the software and how to apply it, you'll then learn how to make NetMeeting benefit your personal and business life.

NetMeeting opens the door to a new way of communication and a new way of doing business. One of the most exciting new methods of communication is talking over the Internet, the subject of the next chapter.

THE INTERNET PHONE

IN THIS CHAPTER YOU LEARN THESE KEY SKILLS

2

One of the most useful features found in NetMeeting is the Internet Phone. You can use this capability to call someone in your office or phone a friend on the other side of the globe — all without paying additional phone charges. This magic is done using Internet Telephony.

Since you were a youngster, you have probably used a telephone. You pick up the receiver, dial the appropriate number, and start talking. Well, now with Internet Telephony, you connect to your service provider, select the appropriate Internet Protocol (IP) address, use NetMeeting to place the call, and start talking. The result is the same; only the method of connecting has changed.

In this chapter, you learn how NetMeeting uses the Internet to place a call. You also learn how to adjust your audio settings for maximum performance, select the Internet Phone feature, and make an Internet phone call.

NOTE   For a preview of a few of the important features you'll find in this chapter, turn to the Discovery Center. You can use the page references in the Discovery Center to quickly find additional information.

Understanding Internet Telephony

Think of the Internet as a worldwide e-mail system. If you have the correct e-mail address, you can send a message to anyone on the planet. You simply connect to your service provider, launch e-mail software, type the recipient's address, type a subject, type your message, and send it. The data you have entered shoots across the globe in search of the e-mail address and then suddenly appears on the recipient's computer — well, most of the time. Just as your text data zooms across the Internet, audio can be digitized and passed through the Internet as well. Internet telephony uses this digitized data to send audio between two or more computers in real time resulting in a conversation, as shown in Figure 2-1.

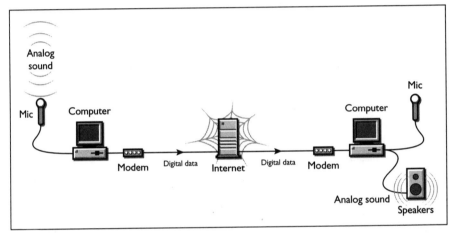

Figure 2-1   How Internet Telephony works.

Internet Telephony software was first introduced in 1995, so the technology is very young. It has endured some growing pains and still has a way to go before it becomes a common way of communication. Microsoft's NetMeeting software will undoubtedly speed this process; however, the Internet Telephony gateway is the key to bringing the technology to the mass market.

The Internet Telephony gateway will bridge the traditional telephone with the Internet. The gateway will take a standard telephone signal and digitize it, compress it, package it for the Internet, and route it to its destination. You can use this service from any telephone in the world to connect to any computer in the world. There are many technical issues and possibilities surrounding Internet Telephony. But for now, comparing an e-mail message with a digital audio message will help you understand how your voice gets from California to France using your computer. If you want to learn the technical details, turn to Appendix B.

Understanding the concept is good, but "doing" is essential to learning. The remainder of this chapter guides you through the process of making an Internet phone call via Internet Telephony using NetMeeting.

Tuning Your Audio

The first step toward placing an Internet phone call is adjusting your audio settings. To adjust your audio settings, you must have an appropriate sound card in your computer. If you do not have a sound card, you won't be able to use NetMeeting's Audio Tuning feature. To solve this problem, you can either purchase a sound card or use one of NetMeeting's text or graphic features.

 You can find technical information about sound cards in Appendix B.

 TIP NetMeeting provides a wizard to help you adjust your audio settings. You may need to use some of the advanced options provided in NetMeeting to optimize your performance, but the wizard is a wonderful place to start. So, you're off to see the wizard.

To adjust your audio using the Audio Tuning Wizard, follow these steps:

1. Launch NetMeeting by following the steps outlined in Chapter 1.

2. Click Tools → Audio Tuning Wizard . The result is shown in Figure 2-2.

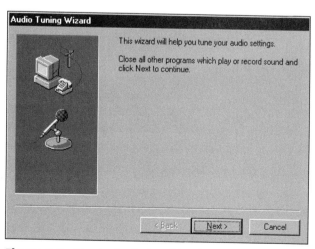

Figure 2-2 The Audio Tuning Wizard.

3. Click the Next button.

4. Click the type of connection you have with your Internet Service Provider, as shown in Figure 2-3.

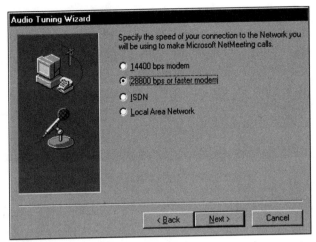

Figure 2-3 Choosing the type of connection used to make NetMeeting calls.

5. Click Next.

6. Click the Start Recording button and read the text aloud to automatically tune your audio settings.

TIP **Be sure that you have your microphone plugged in and placed in its usual position. Don't move the mic closer for the test or talk louder than normal; it will provide a false reading and bad results.**

7. Click Next if you are satisfied with your recording. If you had any trouble reading the text aloud or just want to do it again, click the <Back button and repeat Step 7.

8. The Audio Tuning Wizard informs you that you have completed the tuning. Click the Finish button.

9. If for any reason you have audio problems when using NetMeeting or you move or replace your microphone, simply re-run the Audio Tuning Wizard.

The next process requires that you enable full duplex audio if you have the full duplex capability with your sound card (NetMeeting will detect it automatically and instruct you to enable it if you want). Full duplex enables both parties to speak at the same time, much as a telephone conversation often goes. With half duplex, on the other hand, only one party can speak and be heard at a time.

To enable full duplex if your sound card supports it, follow these steps:

1. Select <kbd>Tools</kbd> → <kbd>Options</kbd> from the menu bar.

2. Choose the Audio tab from the resulting dialog box.

3. Choose the Enable full duplex audio so I can speak while receiving audio option.

4. Click OK.

Addressing a Call

Now that you have successfully tuned the audio portion of your program, you are almost ready to make your first Internet call. First, you need to select the Internet Phone feature and address the call. This procedure is the equivalent of looking up a phone number in the telephone book, writing it down, picking up the receiver, and listening for a dial tone.

To select the Internet Phone Feature and address the call, follow these steps:

1. Choose <kbd>Call</kbd> → <kbd>New Call</kbd> from the menu bar, or click the Call icon on the main toolbar. The New Call dialog box appears, as shown in Figure 2-4.

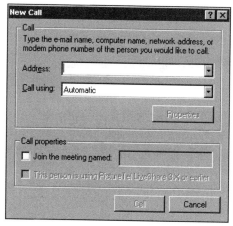

Figure 2-4　The New Call dialog box.

2. In the Address window, type the identity (in most cases, the e-mail address) of the computer you are calling.

TIP If you are calling using the IPX protocol over a network, you would type the computer's IPX address. If you are calling using the TCP/IP protocol over a network or the Internet, you would type either the computer's IP address (the computer's name) or the name of the person listed in the User Location Service Directory. Refer to Appendix B for more detailed information.

3. In the Call using pop-up window, specify whether you are using a modem or a network connection along with the protocol you are using. For now, choose Automatic. Refer to Appendix B for detailed information.

4. Select Join the meeting named: if you want to call a conferencing service. In the option window, type the name of the meeting you want to join. For now, though, do not select this option.

5. Select This person is using PictureTel LiveShare if you know that the person you are calling is running PictureTel LiveShare software.

Making an Internet Call

After you have addressed the call, you are ready to place the call and begin your conference. You can equate this procedure to dialing a traditional phone number, listening as it rings, hearing the person answer, talking, connecting others in a conference call, conducting your meeting, and hanging up.

To make an Internet phone call, follow these steps:

1. Complete the steps for addressing a call and then click Call.

TIP There is an alternative to typing an address in the New Call dialog box. You can simply select and highlight a name from the ULS Directory window. After highlighting the name, click the Call button from the main toolbar. The highlighted name automatically appears in the address window of the New Call dialog box, as shown in Figure 2-5. Click Call and proceed to Step 2.

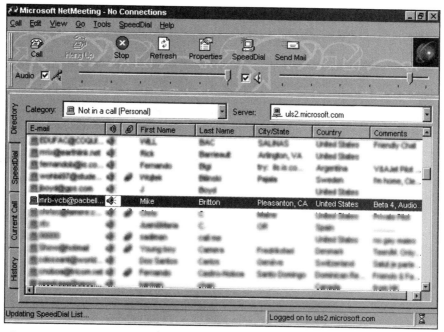

Figure 2-5 The ULS Directory window with the address highlighted in the New Call dialog box.

2. An incoming dialog box appears on the computer of the person you are trying to call. The dialog box (see Figure 2-6) gives the recipient the option of accepting the call or ignoring the call. To answer your call, the person you are calling will click the Accept button.

Figure 2-6 The Incoming Call dialog box of the person you are calling.

3. Upon acceptance of the call, the Current Call window will list you and the person you called. The status bar will show that the person you called has joined the conference, as shown in Figure 2-7. As others enter the conference, their names will be listed in the Current Call window, as shown in Figure 2-8.

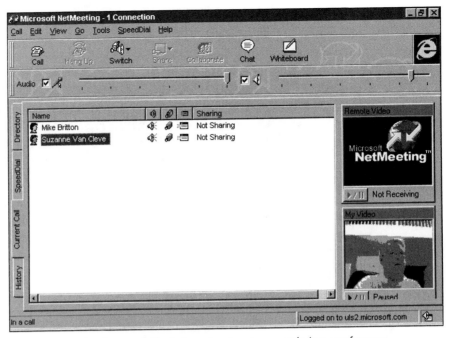

Figure 2-7 The Current Call window showing two people in a conference.

NOTE As you can see in Figure 2-8, the audio and video icons "light up" if the participant has those capabilities. Also shown in the Current Call window are the properties and sharing status of each participant.

4. If you have trouble hearing or your voice is distorted, you can use the Audio toolbar to adjust the microphone and the speaker volume. Move the sliders to the right to increase the volume; move them to the left to decrease the volume. The Audio toolbar is shown in Figure 2-9.

TIP Use the mute boxes, shown in Figure 2-9, to temporarily turn off your microphone or your speakers. When the boxes are checked, the microphone and speakers are on. When they are unchecked, they are off.

TIP If you want to automatically adjust the microphone settings, re-run the Audio Tuning Wizard by choosing ▣ Tools ▣ → ▣ Audio Tuning Wizard ▣ from the menu bar. If you really want to take control and fine-tune your audio settings, adjust the Audio preferences using the NetMeeting Options dialog box and the Advanced Compression Settings shown in Figure 2-10. See the "Bonus" section of this chapter for steps on manually tuning your audio.

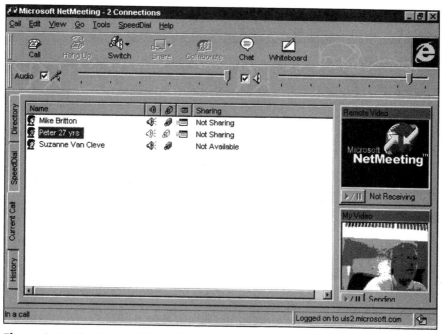

Figure 2-8 The Current Call window showing an additional conference attendee.

Mute buttons

Figure 2-9 The Audio toolbar.

5. After you have made all the necessary adjustments, you are ready to conduct your conversation. Talk into the microphone and listen through the speakers.

 TIP To prevent audio feedback, you can use headphones rather than external speakers. If you are in an office environment, it is less distracting as well. Talking over the Internet can be a little intimidating. You will probably find that using headphones is more natural than broadcasting to your neighbors.

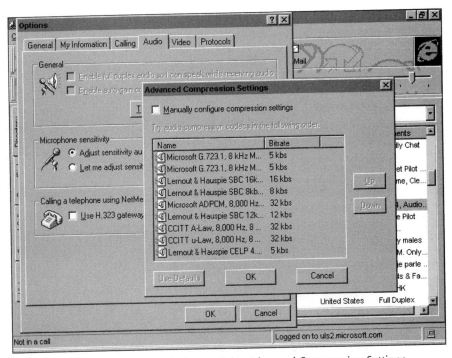

Figure 2-10 The Audio tab window and the Advanced Compression Settings dialog box.

When talking on a standard telephone, you are connected in full duplex mode, meaning both parties can speak at the same time. Some sound cards only support half duplex, meaning that only one party can speak at a time, much like a radio transmission in an old war movie. You know, where the pilot says "We're cleared for landing. Over." Well, the "Over" part of that transmission lets the person on the other end know that the pilot is done talking. A technique such as this might be used to facilitate communication if one person doesn't have full duplex. This method can be awkward and may take some time to master. So give it a try with a friend before you attempt a business conference. For more information on full and half duplex, see Appendix B.

6. To connect another person to the conference, either select a name from the Directory window and click Call from the main toolbar, or click Accept when another person calls you and wants to enter the conference. Refer to Figure 2-8 to see the Current Call window showing three conference attendees.

NetMeeting supports meetings of up to 32 people. However, only the first two people connected with audio can participate in an audio call. All other participants must use a text or graphic feature to communicate. This limitation poses some problems in effective communication. Chapter 8 will help you sort out these issues and provide methods to overcome this problem.

7. When it's time to conclude your call, notify the participants in the conference that you are hanging up and click the Hang Up button from the main toolbar, as shown in Figure 2-11.

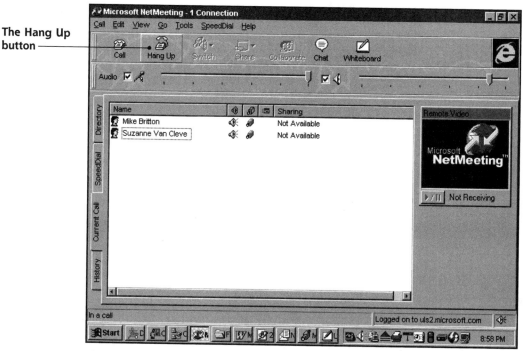

Figure 2-11   To conclude your call, click the Hang Up button.

8. You are now ready to make another call or exit the program. To make another call, just follow the previous instructions in this section. To exit the program, choose Call → Exit from the menu bar.

BONUS

Manually Modifying Audio Settings

First, you must be using a local area network (LAN) or an Internet connection with the TCP/IP protocol to use the audio features of NetMeeting. You cannot take advantage of this feature if you are connected modem-to-modem or if you are using the IPX/SPX connection.

When you run NetMeeting for the first time, you automatically configure your audio setting by using the Audio Tuning Wizard. In addition, you can run the Wizard at any time as described in this chapter. During this tuning, NetMeeting automatically configures your audio compression settings and your microphone sensitivity. The compression level is determined based on your connection speed, and the microphone sensitivity is based on the reading sample that you record when using the wizard.

It is possible to manually configure your audio compression and microphone sensitivity settings if you don't like the result of NetMeeting's wizard. If you are having audio trouble, try manually configuring the settings. If you aren't having trouble, don't worry about understanding this section.

To manually configure your audio compression, follow these steps:

1. Choose `Tools` → `Options` from the menu bar.

2. Click the Audio tab in the NetMeeting Options window. The Audio tab window appears, as shown in Figure 2-12.

3. Click the Advanced button to access the Advanced Compression Settings window, as shown in Figure 2-13. This window lists the audio compression codecs that are available to NetMeeting.

4. Click the Manually configure compression settings check box.

NOTE An audio compression codec converts a sound into a form you can transmit over the Internet.

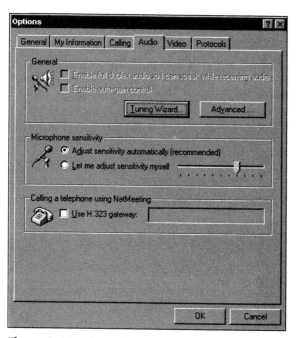

Figure 2-12 The Audio tab window.

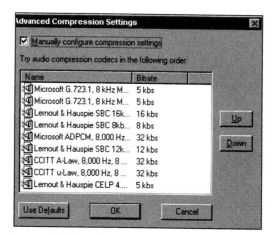

Figure 2-13 The Advanced Compression
Settings window.

5. Click the codec you want to alter. You can move it up in the list or down
by using the Up and Down buttons. You really don't need to understand
how this works, but if you are having problems, changing the order can
help.

6. When you have established a codec order that you're happy with, click
OK. The NetMeeting Options window appears.

7. Click OK to activate your new settings.

To manually configure your microphone sensitivity, follow these steps:

1. Choose Tools → Options from the menu.

2. Click the Audio tab in the NetMeeting Options window. The Audio tab window appears, as shown in Figure 2-12.

3. Click the Let me adjust sensitivity myself radio button.

4. Move the slider to the right to increase the sensitivity of your microphone, or move the slider to the left to decrease the sensitivity of your microphone.

5. Click OK to activate the new setting.

Summary

This chapter covered the basic functions of the Internet Phone feature of NetMeeting. You learned about Internet Telephony and how your voice is translated into digital data that is sent across the Internet just like an e-mail message. You also learned how to choose the Internet Phone feature from the menu bar or main toolbar. You discovered how to address a call, place a call, add a third person to a conference, and hang up. In addition, you learned how to adjust some of the primary audio settings found in NetMeeting.

Practice using the Internet Phone feature. Scroll through the ULS Directory window and read the Comments section. You will undoubtedly find people who are wanting to test their new software. As an alternative, add a comment such as "Please call, I'm testing the audio" to your profile in the Directory tab window. This way, people know it's all right to call you and you have audio capabilities.

Audio is just one way of communicating in NetMeeting. In the next chapter, you discover how to share an application when you're in a conference.

APPLICATION SHARING

IN THIS CHAPTER YOU LEARN THESE KEY SKILLS

SELECTING THE APPLICATION SHARING
   FEATURE   PAGE   48

UNDERSTANDING SHARING AND
   COLLABORATION   PAGE   49

SHARING AN APPLICATION   PAGE   51

3

N etMeeting allows you to share an application that you have running on your computer with others in the conference. Each participant can view the application and, with the proper authorization, take control of it. Programs can be shared even if a participant does not have that particular software application installed on his or her machine. This feature is one of NetMeeting's most powerful and one that is very useful in a business setting (see the "Bonus" section of this chapter).

Application sharing is not new to computing. Since the mid to late '80s, there have been application sharing programs on the market. In the early days, you needed at least four phone lines: two modem lines and two voice lines. You also had to prepare in advance for this type of conference, and you had to pay long-distance charges. In addition, only two parties could share at any one time. With NetMeeting you can talk, see video, write on a whiteboard, and share an application on the same line at the same time and without paying a long-distance phone bill. NetMeeting also supports up to 32 people in a conference, so you can share your applications with nearly three dozen of your closest friends.

In this chapter, you learn the basics of Application Sharing. Later in the book, you'll understand the benefits that Application Sharing can bring to your business life.

NOTE For a preview of a few of the important features you'll find in this chapter, turn to the Discovery Center. You can use the page references in the Discovery Center to quickly find additional information.

Selecting the Application Sharing Feature

Before you can use the Application Sharing feature, you must be running NetMeeting, be connected in a conference, and be running the application you want to share. If you've met all three of these conditions, you can choose the feature.

To choose Application Sharing, follow these steps:

1. Choose **Tools** → **Share Application** from the menu bar, as shown in Figure 3-1. A pop-up menu appears, listing the applications that are available to share.

2. Click the application you want to share.

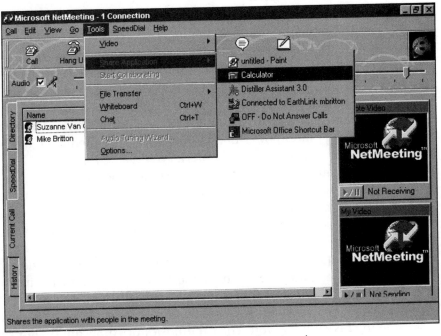

Figure 3-1 Choosing Application Sharing from the menu bar.

Or

1. Click the Share button from the main toolbar, as shown in Figure 3-2. A pop-up menu appears, listing the applications that are available to share.

2. Click the application you want to share.

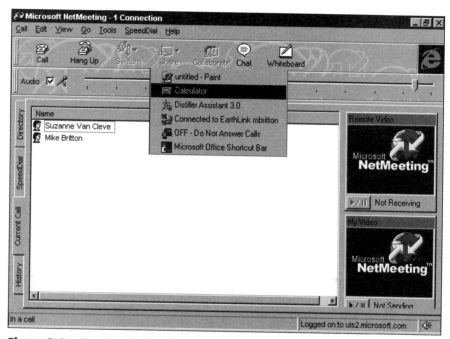

Figure 3-2 Choosing Application Sharing from the main toolbar.

Understanding Application Sharing

Even though there are few preferences to select when using Application Sharing, there are several things to consider before you decide to share an application. For example, when you share control of an application, other participants will be able to use features in that application to control hardware devices such as printers. These participants will also be able to use the application's File Open and File Save dialog boxes to access or delete files from your computer or network.

TIP It is extremely important that you understand the procedures and the risk in sharing your applications. Never share an application with someone you don't know unless you have taken the proper precautions to protect your computer.

What Can You Share?

NetMeeting allows you to share almost any application that you can run on your computer. You can also share folders and windows. For example, if you share Windows Explorer, you will be sharing all of the contents of your computer. In addition, after you have shared a Windows Explorer window, all the applications that you launch during your conference will automatically be shared with each participant. Another example is sharing the My Computer folder. By simply sharing this folder, a remote participant can access the innermost workings of your computer through the Control Panel, as shown in Figure 3-3. So a word of warning: Watch what you share.

Figure 3-3 The Control Panel accessed by a remote NetMeeting participant.

 TIP Don't leave your computer unattended while sharing an application. You may return to find a very undesirable situation.

Potentially, there are some very bad side effects to sharing files. However, in NetMeeting you can always be in control of the situation and never have a problem if you know what you're doing. The rest of this chapter teaches you how to share files and be safe.

Working Alone or Collaborating

When sharing an application, NetMeeting gives you the choice of working alone or collaborating. In other words, if you choose to share an application, you can also choose whether or not to give control of that application to the remote participants. Whenever you select the Application Sharing feature, the default setting is working alone — that is, you have complete control, and the others can only view what you do. You must actively choose to share control of the application by collaborating, which gives the remote participants the ability to control the activity. Simply click the Collaborate button on the main toolbar to share control of your application. The dialog box shown in Figure 3-4 appears. Click OK.

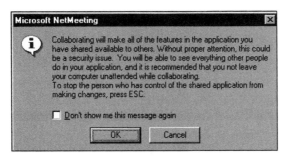

Figure 3-4 The Collaborating dialog box.

TIP If you have given control of your application to a remote participant and for some reason find yourself out of control, you can regain control at any time. To stop someone from controlling your shared program while they have control of the cursor, press Esc. This brings back control of the application to you.

If you want to stop someone from controlling your shared program while you have control of the cursor, click the Work Alone button on the main toolbar.

Sharing an Application

By now you know how to select the Application Sharing feature, and you have read about the problems that can arise when giving control of your computer to a complete stranger.

Given this danger, you're probably wondering why anyone would ever use this function. The answer is simple — it is a very powerful tool. Using the Application Sharing feature in business can reduce cost and facilitate decision making. Using it in a personal setting can be fun and rewarding as well, as long as you know how to do it.

X-REF For more information on using the Application Sharing feature to benefit your business, see Chapter 14.

To use the Application Sharing feature, follow these steps:

1. Launch NetMeeting and connect to a ULS server, as described in Chapter 1.

2. Address and connect to a conference participant, as described in Chapter 2.

3. Inform the remote participant that you are going to share an application. If you are in a voice call, you can achieve this using the Internet Phone feature. If you have more than one participant or you are not using the audio features of NetMeeting, you can use the Chat or Whiteboard feature.

 For more information on using the Chat and Whiteboard features, see Chapter 5 and Chapter 6.

4. Choose ⎡ **Tools** ⎤ → ⎡ **Share Application** ⎤ from the menu bar, as shown in the top panel of Figure 3-5. Or click the Share button in the main toolbar as shown in the bottom panel of Figure 3-5. A pop-up menu appears, listing the applications that are available to share.

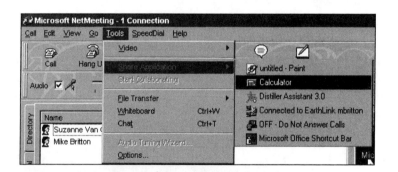

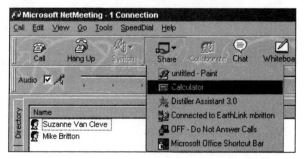

Figure 3-5   Choosing the Application Sharing feature from the menu bar (top) and the main toolbar (bottom).

5. Click the application or window that you want to share. For this
   example, the Calculator application has been chosen. The dialog box
   shown in Figure 3-6 appears.

6. Click OK.

Figure 3-6 The Sharing dialog box.

7. Bring the shared window or application to the front. To do so, click the
   application icon in the Windows status bar, as shown in Figure 3-7. The
   remote participant(s) must also click the application icon. (*Note:* The
   application is seen on every computer in the conference. The name of
   the program's owner is displayed in the upper-right corner of the
   window.)

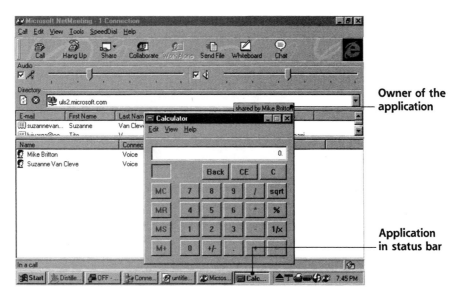

Owner of the
application

Application
in status bar

Figure 3-7 Bringing the Shared Application
window to the front using the
Windows status bar.

TIP The active window of a program being shared appears on the computer of the remote participant. Remember, when a program is shared, the entire window is "reflected" on the remote monitor. If part or all of the shared window is covered with a nonshared window, a graphic pattern appears on the remote computer. Keep this in mind when you are conducting a conference using the Application Sharing feature. Otherwise, the remote participants will see the graphic pattern shown in Figure 3-8 rather than the intended application.

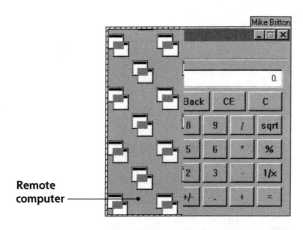

Remote computer

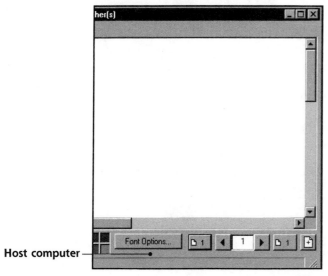

Host computer

Figure 3-8 A graphic pattern on the remote computer (top) represents an area that is covered by the Whiteboard on the host computer (bottom).

Collaborate

8. Decide whether you will allow remote participants to control your application. If yes, click Collaborate in the main toolbar. The Collaborate dialog box appears.

9. Click OK.

10. Arrange your desktop space so that you can access other NetMeeting features. Remember that any window covering the Shared Application window will result in a graphic pattern on the remote computer.

11. The name of the participant controlling the application is shown next to the cursor. If you are not in control of your application, double-click the Shared Application window to take control of the cursor. The sharing status of each participant is shown in the Connection area of the main NetMeeting window.

12. Text or graphics cut or copied from applications can be pasted into the shared application, as shown in Figure 3-9. Choose Edit → Paste from the menu bar.

Figure 3-9 Text is pasted into the Calculator application using the Edit → Paste command.

13. Choose Tools → Share Application from the menu bar to end the Application Sharing feature.

14. Click the application you want to stop sharing. Remember that you can share multiple applications at any time. Just follow the steps listed in this section.

15. Inform the participants that the conference is over.

16. Choose `Call` → `Hang Up` from the menu bar or click the Hang Up button on the main toolbar.

BONUS

Using NetMeeting to Prepare and Present a Budget

The Application Sharing feature can be a wonderful tool in preparing and explaining a budget. It's not uncommon in today's global society for sales managers and finance managers to be in different parts of the country if not the world. In the past, the only way to overcome this problem was to use a system such as Federal Express or commercial airline travel. This, of course, would take time and could be a costly effort. In recent history, the budget numbers could be e-mailed from one place to another. This solved the time issue, but there still was no way for collaboration. A business trip was usually the answer, again a costly proposition.

NetMeeting solves this problem. Consider the following scenario:

You are a sales manager in San Francisco preparing your budget for the CFO in Denver. Your financial manager is across the country in New York. There are some last-minute sales figures that need to be added to the budget before your budget presentation, which, by the way, is tomorrow afternoon in Denver. You also want a discussion with your financial manager to develop some final projections before you stand before the CFO and plead your case. Figure 3-10 shows your Excel spreadsheet missing a few key pieces of information that the financial manager has in New York. What do you do?

- ✳ Take the red-eye to New York, meet the financial manager for breakfast, finalize your budget, run to the airport, fly to Denver for the afternoon presentation. Cost: $2,000.

- ✳ Update information, fax, e-mail spreadsheets, phone conference; update information, fax, e-mail spreadsheets, phone conference; update information, fax, e-mail spreadsheets, phone conference, and so on. Fly to Denver for the afternoon presentation. Cost: $1,000.

- ✳ Use NetMeeting to meet with the financial manager and update the spreadsheet in real time (see Figure 3-11), get a good night's sleep, play a round of golf in the morning, use NetMeeting to present the budget in the afternoon. Cost: none for the budget; $75.00 for greens fees.

Well, this scenario might be a little overstated, but NetMeeting can solve many business problems with its unique blend of communications technology. Use the steps found in this chapter to prepare and present your next budget.

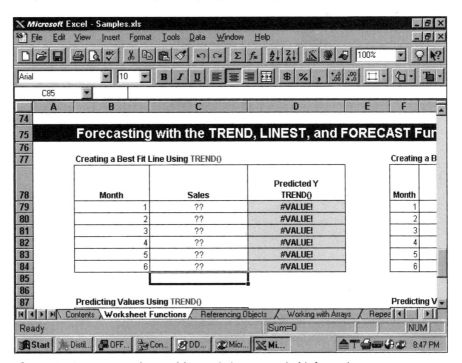

Figure 3-10 Your Excel spreadsheet missing some vital information.

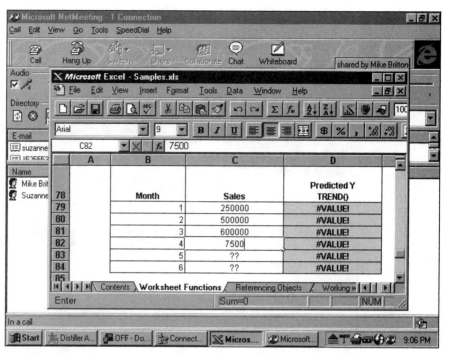

Figure 3-11   Your Excel spreadsheet being updated in NetMeeting.

Summary

This chapter covered the basic functions of the Application Sharing feature. You learned how to select Application Sharing and share a program running on your computer. You determined whether you should allow remote participants to control your computer and what to do to take control back from a remote participant. You also learned how to use the shared clipboard, arrange your workspace, and end sharing an application.

Practice sharing applications with friends. Try sharing a simple application like the Calculator program shown in this chapter. Advanced techniques for effectively using Application Sharing are discussed in later chapters, but as always, you must learn to walk before you run.

CHAPTER FOUR

FILE TRANSFERS

IN THIS CHAPTER YOU LEARN THESE KEY SKILLS

SETTING THE FILE TRANSFER
PREFERENCES PAGE 60

UNDERSTANDING FILE TRANSFERS PAGE 62

TRANSFERRING A FILE TO ALL
PARTICIPANTS PAGE 63

RECEIVING A FILE PAGE 65

TRANSFERRING A FILE TO ONE
PARTICIPANT PAGE 66

4

The file transfer capability of NetMeeting, while not the most glamorous feature, is nonetheless a very useful one. You can transfer a copy of any file on your computer to one or all participants in a conference. You can do this in the "background" so you can continue with your conference while the file speeds its way to its destination.

File Transfer is a much better alternative than the traditional method of attaching a file to an e-mail message. Later in this chapter you'll understand why. Also in this chapter you learn the basics of transferring a file in NetMeeting, and in future chapters you will understand how to use File Transfer to benefit your business.

NOTE For a preview of a few of the important features you'll find in this chapter, turn to the Discovery Center. You can use the page references in the Discovery Center to quickly find additional information.

Setting the File Transfer Preferences

Y ou can find the File Transfer preferences in the General NetMeeting Options window. To access this window, choose **Options** from the **Tools** menu on the menu bar. The NetMeeting Options window appears, as shown in Figure 4-1. The General tab is the default.

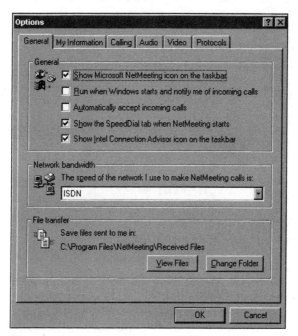

Figure 4-1 The NetMeeting Options window.

To set the preferences for File Transfer, follow these steps:

1. Choose **Tools** → **Options** from the menu bar. The NetMeeting Options window appears.

2. Find the File transfer section located at the bottom of the window. You will see two buttons, labeled View Files and Change Folder.

3. Click the Change Folder button to specify the folder on your computer where you want incoming files to be saved. The default setting is C:\Program Files\NetMeeting\Received Files. The Browse for Folder window appears, as shown in Figure 4-2.

4. Select the appropriate folder in the directory hierarchy. Figure 4-3 shows that the transferred files will be sent to the My Documents folder.

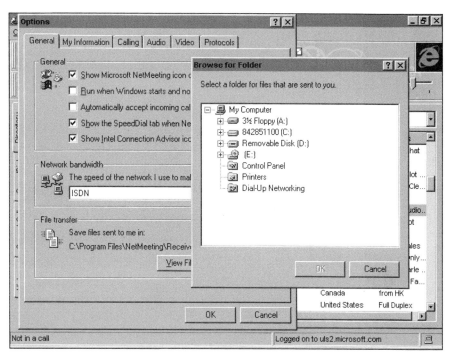

Figure 4-2 The Browse for Folder window.

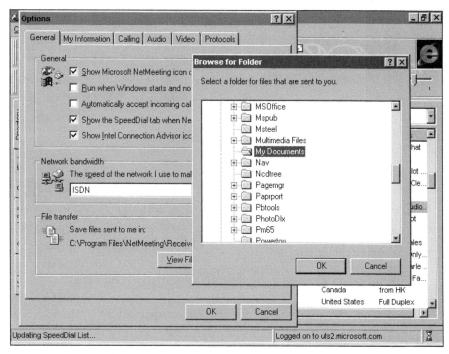

Figure 4-3 Choosing the My Documents folder.

5. Click the OK button in the Browse for Folder window to set the new destination for transferred files.

6. Click the OK button in the NetMeeting Options window to save your preferences.

Understanding File Transfers

I f you have ever attached and sent a file from your e-mail account, you already understand the basics of file transfers. If this is a foreign subject, this section should help you understand some of the issues about sending digital files across the Internet.

What Is File Transfer?

In the simplest of terms, file transfer is the act of sending a copy of a file that resides on one computer to another computer. You can accomplish this transfer by doing one of the following tasks:

* Copying a file to a diskette and transferring the diskette from one computer to another.

* Attaching a file to an e-mail message and uploading the message, with the attachment, to an e-mail provider. The message is sent across the Internet and then downloaded by the receiving computer.

* Copying a file "directly" from one computer to another over a local area network (LAN) or wide area network (WAN) using proprietary networking software such as Novell NetWare.

* Copying a file "directly" from one computer to another or to several computers by using NetMeeting.

Advantages of NetMeeting's File Transfer

There are several advantages of using NetMeeting to transfer your files. Unless you are near the receiving computer where sneaker netting a diskette is the way to go, the File Transfer feature will save you time and money.

For example, using the diskette method to transfer a file across the country entails an expense for the diskette and a shipping cost that could be substantial if sent as a priority overnight package. Using a LAN or WAN to transfer files is easy, but you must have the expensive infrastructure in place and your recipients are limited to only those with network access. Using the e-mail approach has many complications, including uploading and downloading time. In addition, the attachment goes through several gateways and in some cases doesn't arrive intact after the time has been spent to upload and download.

NetMeeting combines the benefits of a direct transfer with the global network of anyone who has an Internet connection. The transfer happens in the "background" so you can continue to communicate with audio, video, or any other NetMeeting feature and eliminate the upload and download issue. Because the NetMeeting transfer happens while connected to your Internet Service Provider (ISP), you don't have to pay any additional on-line fees such as with America Online (AOL).

To take advantage of NetMeeting's File Transfer benefits, you need to know the proper steps to follow when transferring a file. The next section shows you how to do just that.

Transferring a File to All Participants

By now you know how to select the File Transfer preferences and you understand in basic terms the process that NetMeeting uses to transfer a file. Now it's time to get on with transferring a file.

To send a file to all participants, follow these steps:

1. Launch NetMeeting and connect to a ULS server, as described in Chapter 1.

2. Address and connect to a conference participant, as described in Chapter 2.

3. Inform the remote participant(s) that you are going to transfer a file. If you are in a voice call, you can achieve this using the Internet Phone feature (refer to Chapter 2). If you have more than one participant or you are not using the Audio feature of NetMeeting, you can use the Chat or Whiteboard feature.

 For more information on using the Chat and Whiteboard features, see Chapters 5 and 6.

4. Choose Tools → File Transfer → Send File , as shown in Figure 4-4. The Select a File to Send window appears, as shown in Figure 4-5.

5. Using the Windows directory hierarchy, choose a file to send by using the pop-up menu to navigate to the appropriate file.

6. Click the file you want to send, as shown in Figure 4-6.

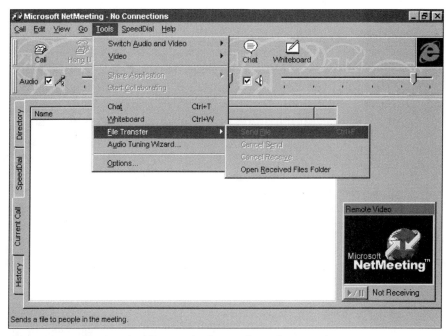

Figure 4-4 Selecting the File Transfer feature from the menu bar.

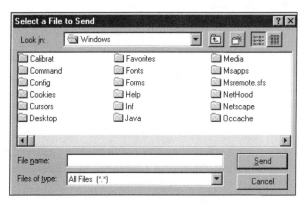

Figure 4-5 The Select a File to Send window.

7. Click the Send button. The file is sent to all the participants in the conference.

8. Click OK and the file transfer is complete.

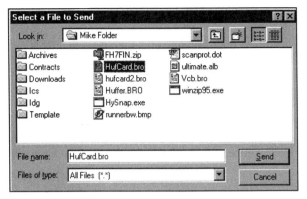

Figure 4-6 Choosing a file to transfer.

Receiving a File

Now that you know how to transfer a file to another participant, you can read this section to learn about how to receive and open a file.

To receive a file using the File Transfer feature, follow these steps:

1. Launch NetMeeting and connect to a ULS server, as described in Chapter 1.

2. Address and connect to a conference participant, as described in Chapter 2.

3. A participant informs you that a file is being transferred and the Virus-Warning dialog box shown in Figure 4-7 appears. The Virus-Warning dialog box informs you that a file is being received. It also indicates where the file is being saved, whom it is from, how big the file is, and it proclaims a warning about viruses.

Figure 4-7 The Virus-Warning dialog box.

4. Choose one of the three options offered by the Virus-Warning dialog box:

> Click Close to close the window and store the file.

> Click Open to open the folder where the file has been transferred.

Or,

> Click Delete to remove the transferred file from your computer.

Transferring a File to One Participant

You may have an occasion when you want to transfer a file to only one participant in a multiperson conference. If this occurs, simply follow the instructions in this section.

To send a file to only one participant, follow these steps:

1. Launch NetMeeting and connect to a ULS server, as described in Chapter 1.

2. Address and connect to a conference participant, as described in Chapter 2.

3. Inform the remote participant that you are going to transfer a file.

4. In the Connection window, right-click the name of the participant to whom you want to send the file. A menu appears, as shown in Figure 4-8. Choose Send File .

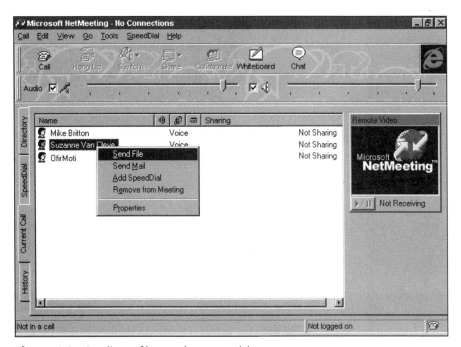

Figure 4-8   Sending a file to only one participant.

5. Using the Windows directory hierarchy, choose a file to send by using the pop-up menu to navigate to the appropriate file.

6. Click the file you want to send.

7. Click the Send button. The file is sent to only the participant you chose.

8. Click OK and the file transfer is complete.

BONUS

Using File Transfer and Adobe Acrobat to Proof a Document

Using the File Transfer feature of NetMeeting can save you and your company precious time and dollars, as discussed in this chapter. File Transfer can also facilitate the proofing process of almost any business document.

Remember back to the old days, you know, a couple of years ago. To proof a paper document in those days, you would first print the document and then route the paper to as many people as needed for input. Each person would mark comments and corrections with a different colored pen and then send the paper to the next person on the list. After a few weeks, the document would find its way back to you. You would analyze the hieroglyphics trying to discern their meaning and update the file as needed, then start the proofing process all over again.

Well, with File Transfer from NetMeeting and Acrobat from Adobe, you can simplify this process.

WEB PATH **Visit this Web site for more information about Adobe Acrobat and the .PDF file format.**

`http://www.adobe.com/acrobat/`

To proof a document using NetMeeting and Acrobat, follow these steps:

1. Save the electronic document as a .PDF file, as shown in Figure 4-9.

NOTE Adobe Systems created the .PDF file format, which allows you to exchange documents with people regardless of the type of computer they have or the software they use. Although Acrobat files cannot be altered, the format does allow you to enter comments on electronic "sticky notes" and compile these comments for easy proofing.

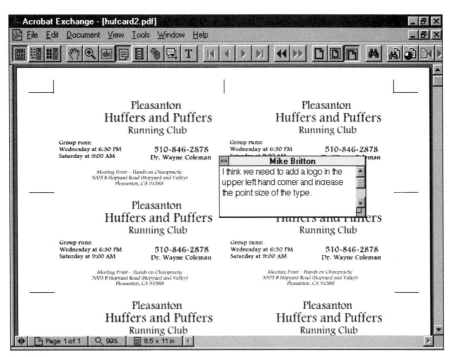

Figure 4-9 A .PDF file showing the Notes feature of Adobe Acrobat.

2. Enter into a NetMeeting conference with all the participants that need to proof the document.

3. Explain to the participants any background information about the document.

4. Follow the instructions in this chapter to transfer a copy of the files to each participant.

5. Instruct each participant to review the document and use the Notes feature of Acrobat to record comments and changes.

6. After the comments have been added, instruct each participant to right-click your name and transfer the proofed document to your Receive Folder.

7. End the NetMeeting conference.

8. Use the Compile Notes feature of Adobe Acrobat to assemble all the comments and revise as needed.

TIP As an alternative to the File Transfer feature, you could use Application Sharing (explained in Chapter 3) to get group feedback. Choose the best method or use a combination of both.

Summary

This chapter covered the basic function of NetMeeting's File Transfer feature. You learned how to set the preferences, transfer a file to everyone in the conference, receive a file, and send a file to only one person in the conference. Understanding the functions is the first step. Putting that knowledge to use is the next. Chapters 9, 10, 11, and 12 discuss creative ways of using File Transfer to benefit your personal and business life.

The File Transfer feature is a very useful tool in combination with other NetMeeting features. Turn to the next chapter to learn about the most creative feature in NetMeeting, the Whiteboard.

CHAPTER FIVE

THE
WHITEBOARD

IN THIS CHAPTER YOU LEARN THESE KEY SKILLS

The Whiteboard is NetMeeting's most creative feature. Whether you are a novice artist or a Picasso, you'll find the Whiteboard's capabilities fun and very useful. The Whiteboard allows you to express yourself in ways that the written word (Chat), voice (Internet Phone), or video (Video Conference) can't achieve.

Although the Whiteboard is not as sophisticated as most illustration programs, such as Adobe Illustrator, it sports the following useful communication tools:

* Drawing Pen
* Highlight tool
* Line tool
* Rectangle and Circle tool
* Zoom tool
* Eraser
* Remote Pointer
* Text tool

In addition, you can cut and paste objects into the Whiteboard and, because it is object-oriented like Adobe Illustrator, not pixel-oriented like Microsoft Paint, you can move and manipulate objects by clicking with the mouse and dragging.

In this chapter, you learn the basics of the Whiteboard along with some helpful tips on how to use this creative communication tool. You also learn how to create effective graphics using this tool.

NOTE For a preview of a few of the important features you'll find in this chapter, turn to the Discovery Center. You can use the page references in the Discovery Center to quickly find additional information.

So, You Want to Use the Whiteboard

To access most of NetMeeting's features, you must first be in a conference; but this is not true of the Whiteboard. You can launch, run, and draw as much as you like without being connected to your ULS.

Follow one of these four options to select the Whiteboard:

1. Choose Tools → Whiteboard from the menu bar, as shown in Figure 5-1.

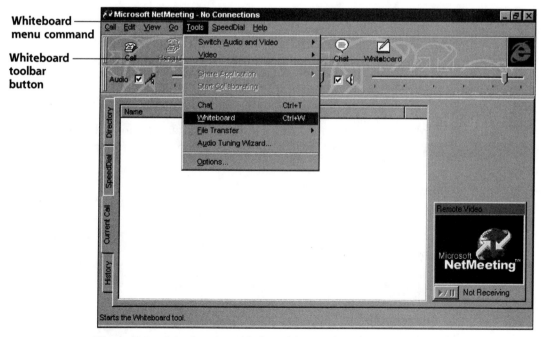

Whiteboard menu command

Whiteboard toolbar button

Figure 5-1 Selecting the Whiteboard feature from the menu bar.

2. Click the Whiteboard icon on the main toolbar.

3. Press Control+W.

4. Click the NetMeeting icon in the taskbar and then click the Whiteboard button, as shown in Figure 5-2.

 Figure 5-2 Selecting the Whiteboard feature from the taskbar.

If It Doesn't Fit, Adjust It!

To select the Whiteboard, use one of the four methods just described. The main Whiteboard window appears, as shown in Figure 5-3. From this window (not the main NetMeeting window), adjust the Whiteboard settings. You can choose from two general preferences that deal with hiding and displaying the toolbar and status bar. You can also choose from three object-oriented settings that allow you to change the color palette, the fonts, and the width of a line. All of these settings can be changed at any time.

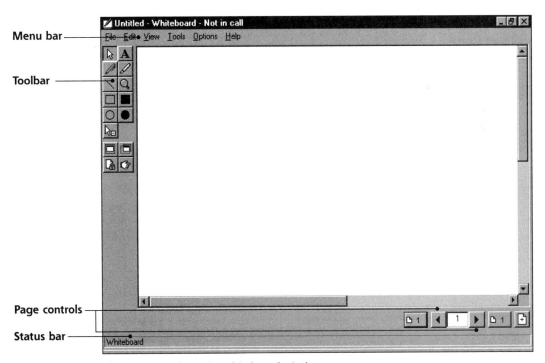

Figure 5-3 The main Whiteboard window.

Follow these steps to adjust the general preferences:

1. Choose   View   →   Tool Bar   to display or hide the toolbar, as shown in
   Figure 5-4. Click   Tool Bar   in the menu to toggle on and off.

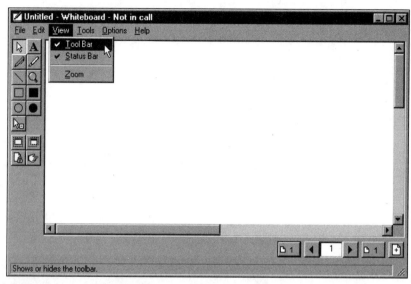

Figure 5-4   Displaying the Tool Bar from the View menu.

2. Choose   View   →   Status Bar   to display or hide the status bar. Click
     Status Bar   in the menu to toggle on and off.

Follow these steps to change the color palette:

1. Click any of the drawing tools. For now, though, click the Draw Tool and
   the color palette shown in Figure 5-5 appears.

2. Choose   Options   →   Colors   to display the Color Selector window, as
   shown in Figure 5-6.

3. Click Define Custom Colors >> and the Color Selector window expands,
   as shown in Figure 5-7.

Draw tool

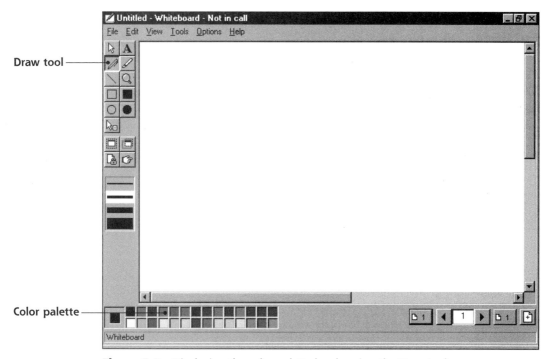

Color palette

Figure 5-5 Displaying the color palette by choosing the Draw tool.

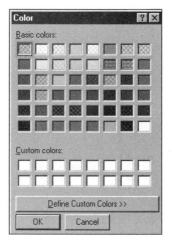

Figure 5-6 The Color Selector window.

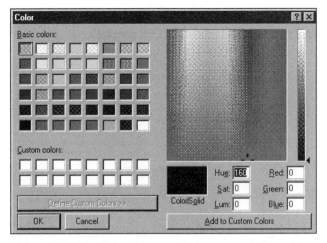

Figure 5-7 The Color Selector window expanded to add custom colors.

4. Click in the color matrix on the custom color you want to add, as shown in Figure 5-8.

5. Move the slider up or down to adjust the levels of black and white in the chosen color, also shown in Figure 5-8.

6. Click Add to Custom Colors and the new color appears in the custom colors palette on the left side of the window, as shown in Figure 5-9.

SIDE TRIP

HUE, SATURATION, AND WHAT?

NetMeeting allows you to choose custom colors three different ways; however, two of them are not very intuitive. In fact, unless you are a serious artist or mix paint for a living, they probably won't make any sense at all.

For example, you can change the values in the Hue, Saturation, and Luminosity boxes. Hue is the value of a color wheel, where 0 is red, 60 is yellow, 120 is green, 180 is cyan, 200 is magenta, and 240 is blue. Saturation is the amount of color in a specified hue, up to a maximum of 240. Luminosity is the brightness of the color. A combination of hue, saturation, and luminosity defines a new color. This information, while accurate, is not very useful. The same goes for the Red, Green, and Blue method. It just doesn't make sense to take the time to learn them.

The easiest method for defining a custom color is the one detailed in this section — the color matrix and the slider. Unless you are trying to match a corporate logo color, you may never have the need to create a custom color in NetMeeting, but the capability is there if you do.

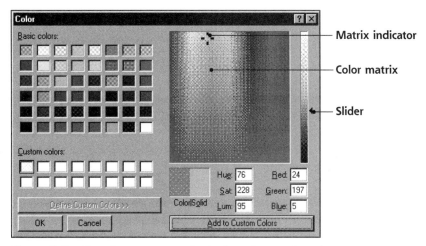

Figure 5-8 Choosing a custom color in the color matrix and adjusting the color with the slider.

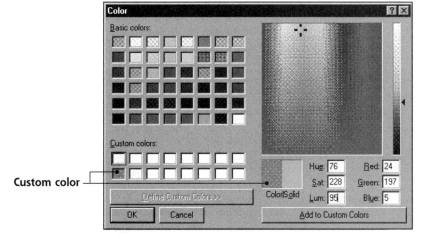

Figure 5-9 Custom color added to the palette.

NOTE The color shade that is shown on the left side of the Color/Solid window is the color that NetMeeting will add to the custom color palette when you click Add to Custom Colors. If you want to add the solid color, press Alt+O and the color shade will become the solid color. Click Add to Custom Colors and the solid color will become part of the custom color palette.

7. Click OK to exit the Color Selector window.

Follow these steps to change the font:

1. Click the Text tool in the toolbar, as shown in Figure 5-10, and the Font Options button appears next to the color palette.

Text tool ——

Font Options —— button

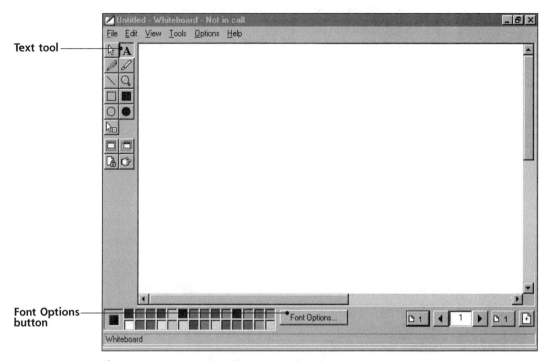

Figure 5-10   Displaying the Font Options button.

2. Click the Font Options button to access the Font dialog box shown in Figure 5-11.

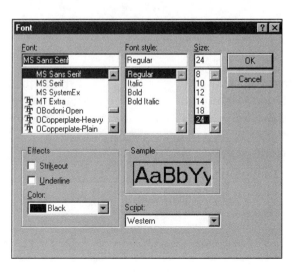

Figure 5-11   The Font dialog box.

3. Click the font, font style, size, effect, and color you want to display on the Whiteboard. An example of your selection is shown in the sample window.

4. Click OK to return to the main Whiteboard window.

Follow these steps to adjust the width of a line:

1. Click the Line Tool as shown in Figure 5-12, and the line width selector appears under the toolbar.

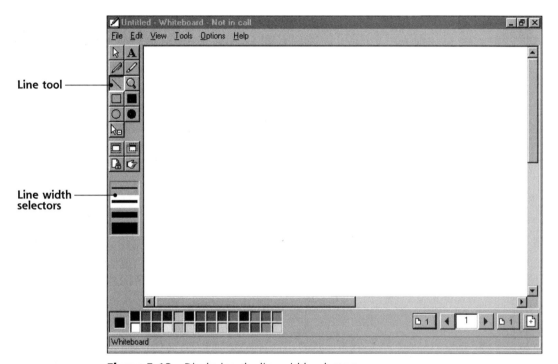

Figure 5-12   Displaying the line width selectors.

NOTE   As an alternative, you can choose Options → Line Width from the menu bar and make your line width selection there instead of choosing the Line Tool. Both methods work the same; it's simply up to your preference.

2. Click the line width you want. That width will remain the default for boxes, circles, and other shapes until you choose another width.

Just What Is the Whiteboard, Anyway?

The Whiteboard is a multipage, multiuser drawing application. You can sketch diagrams and flowcharts, and you can display a variety of graphic information.

Pixel-oriented Versus Object-oriented

As mentioned earlier, the Whiteboard is object-oriented as opposed to pixel-oriented. To illustrate the difference, see Figure 5-13. The illustration on the bottom was created in Microsoft Paint, a pixel-oriented program. The illustration on the top was created on the Whiteboard. Notice the smooth edges on the Whiteboard illustration and the ability to select an entire shape. The pixel-oriented illustration has jagged edges and must be manipulated pixel by pixel. Graphics drawn on the Whiteboard look much better than those drawn in a pixel-oriented program.

Collaborative Artwork

When one participant in a conference chooses the Whiteboard, it appears on all computers. Everyone in the conference can draw on the Whiteboard simultaneously. This can be fun, but could lead to mass confusion. If you do not want other participants to draw on the Whiteboard, simply lock the contents and only you can draw. To lock the contents, click the Lock icon on the toolbar, as shown in Figure 5-14. A dialog box appears to indicate that the Whiteboard is locked. The icon remains depressed to further indicate that you have complete control of the Whiteboard. To unlock the Whiteboard, click the Lock icon once more.

Freedom to Resize

When an application is shared in NetMeeting, the size of the shared window remains the same on all computers. For example, if someone minimizes the shared window, the window is minimized on everyone's screen. This is not the case with the Whiteboard. Each participant can resize, minimize, or maximize the Whiteboard window independent of the other participants. This makes the Whiteboard feature a more effective tool in a large conference.

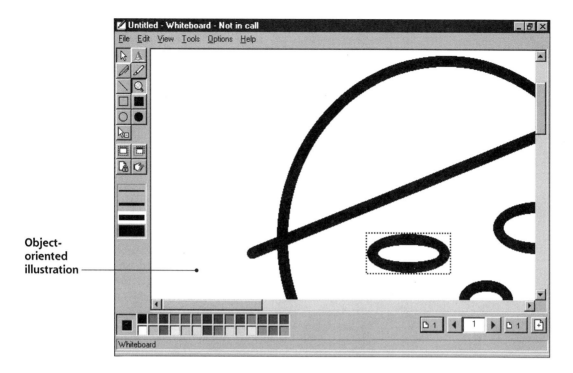

Object-oriented illustration

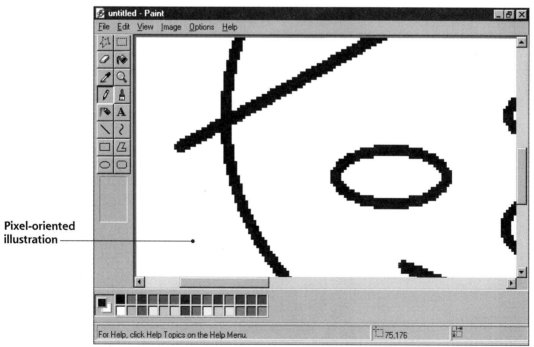

Pixel-oriented illustration

Figure 5-13 An illustration created on the Whiteboard (top) and in Microsoft Paint (bottom).

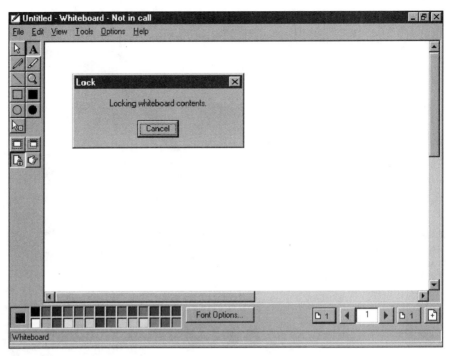

Figure 5-14 Locking the Whiteboard.

Refresh Yourself at the Toolbar

The toolbar is the master control center of the Whiteboard. It contains 15 icons, as shown in Figure 5-15 and described in Table 5-1.

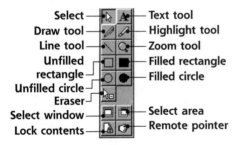

Select ———— Text tool
Draw tool ———— Highlight tool
Line tool ———— Zoom tool
Unfilled rectangle ———— Filled rectangle
Unfilled circle ———— Filled circle
Eraser
Select window ———— Select area
Lock contents ———— Remote pointer

Figure 5-15 The toolbar.

TABLE 5-1   The Toolbar

Button	Name	Description
	Select	Selects an object either by clicking or marqueeing
	Text Tool	Adds text to the Whiteboard
	Draw Tool	Enables freehand drawing
	Highlight Tool	Adds a transparent highlight
	Line Tool	Draws a straight line
	Zoom Tool	Zooms the document up and down
	Unfilled Rectangle	Draws an unfilled rectangle
	Filled Rectangle	Draws a rectangle filled with the chosen color
	Unfilled Circle	Draws an unfilled circle
	Filled Circle	Draws a circle filled with the chosen color
	Eraser	Deletes objects
	Select Window	Pastes the window you select on the Whiteboard
	Select Area	Pastes a marqueed area on the Whiteboard
	Lock Contents	Locks the contents of the Whiteboard
	Remote Pointer	Adds a pointer to the Whiteboard

The functionality of the toolbar is divided into the following five categories and illustrated in Figure 5-16:

* Text
* Graphics
* Management
* Highlighting
* Advanced

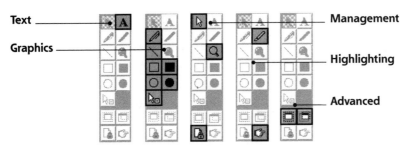

Figure 5-16 The toolbar divided into five categories.

The Document Window

After you choose the Whiteboard feature, the document window appears, as shown in Figure 5-17. The elements of the document window include scroll bars on the bottom and right side of the window. These scroll bars allow you to move around the document window.

Because the Whiteboard is a multipage drawing program, you need a navigation system. The page controls are located in the lower-right corner of the document window. These controls allow you to see how many pages you have created and what page you are currently using. In addition, these controls allow you to move between the pages. Table 5-2 describes each control.

In addition to the page controls, the Whiteboard has a great feature called the Page Sorter. To access the Page Sorter, choose **Page Sorter** from the **Edit** menu on the menu bar, and the window shown in Figure 5-18 appears. From the Page Sorter window, you can insert a page, delete a page, and go to a specific page. Simply click the icon of the page you want to affect, and then click the appropriate button.

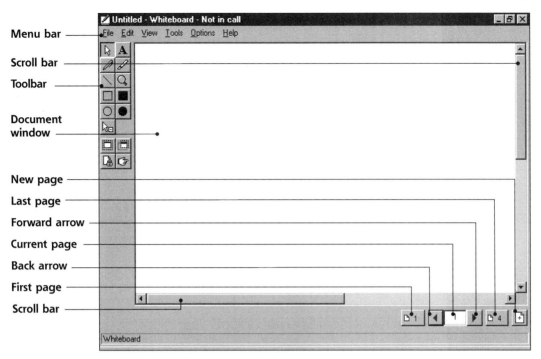

Menu bar

Scroll bar

Toolbar

Document
window

New page

Last page

Forward arrow

Current page

Back arrow

First page

Scroll bar

Figure 5-17 The document window.

TABLE 5-2 Page Controls

Button	Name	Description
🗋 1	First Page	Displays the first page of the Whiteboard document
◀	Back Arrow	Displays the previous page
1	Current Page Box	Indicates the current Whiteboard page
▶	Forward Arrow	Displays the next page
🗋 4	Last Page	Displays the last page of the Whiteboard document
⊕	New Page	Adds a new page to the Whiteboard

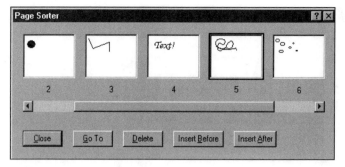

Figure 5-18 The Page Sorter window.

Doin' It on the Whiteboard

So far you have learned to select the Whiteboard and adjust the preferences. You've also learned some of the basic information about the Whiteboard. Now it's time to look at each feature in more detail.

Adding Text to the Whiteboard

Although the Whiteboard is a drawing program and primarily designed for graphic communication, it does have the capability to display textual information.

To add text to the Whiteboard, follow these steps:

1. Click the Text Tool on the toolbar.

2. Adjust the Font Options, as described earlier in this chapter.

3. Click the cursor in the document window.

 NOTE When you select the Text Tool and move the cursor into the document window, the cursor changes shape. It now looks like an I-beam. This transformation is the indication that you have the ability to add text.

4. Type your message into the document window, as shown in Figure 5-19.

To move text that you have added, follow these steps:

1. Click the Select tool on the toolbar.

2. Highlight and hold the text you have typed in the document window.

3. Drag with the mouse to position the text.

4. Release the mouse and the text is repositioned.

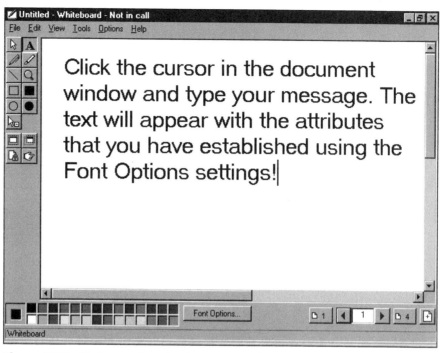

Figure 5-19 Typing text into the document window.

To edit text that exists in the document window, follow these steps:

1. Click the Text tool on the toolbar.

2. Position the cursor in the text block where you want to begin your edit and click.

3. Use the Backspace key to delete text, or type to add text.

To change the font attributes of existing text, follow these steps:

1. Click the Text tool on the toolbar.

2. Click in the text block.

3. Click Font Options and follow the steps described earlier in this chapter.

Sketching It Out

NetMeeting provides four drawing tools in the Whiteboard toolbar:

* Draw tool
* Line tool
* Rectangle tool (unfilled and filled)
* Circle tool (unfilled and filled)

Follow these steps to create a freehand drawing:

1. Click the Draw tool on the toolbar.

2. Adjust the line width, as described earlier in this chapter.

3. Click a color from the color palette at the bottom of the document window, or use the color selector to create a custom color.

4. Move the cursor into the document window.

5. Click and hold while dragging the mouse, as shown in Figure 5-20.

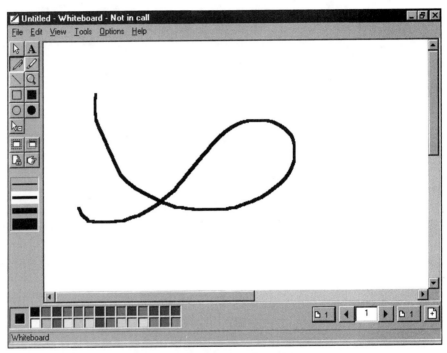

Figure 5-20 The Draw tool drawing a freehand graphic.

6. Release the mouse when you have finished your drawing.

 TIP Using the mouse to draw freehand text is quite difficult, even for an accomplished artist. When trying to convey a textual message, use the Text tool. Otherwise, your Whiteboard will probably look like it was drawn by a toddler.

Follow these steps to draw straight lines:

1. Click the Line tool on the toolbar.

2. Adjust the line width, as described earlier in this chapter.

3. Click a color from the color palette at the bottom of the document window, or use the color selector to create a custom color.

4. Move the cursor into the document window.

5. Click and hold while dragging the mouse, as shown in Figure 5-21.

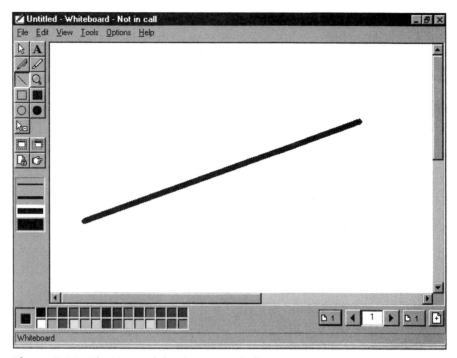

Figure 5-21 The Line tool drawing a straight line.

6. Release the mouse when you have finished drawing the line.

Follow these steps to draw a rectangle:

1. Click the Rectangle tool on the toolbar. Choose either the filled or unfilled rectangle.

2. Adjust the line width, as described earlier in this chapter.

3. Click a color from the color palette at the bottom of the document window, or use the color selector to create a custom color.

4. Move the cursor into the document window.

5. Click and hold while dragging the mouse, as shown in Figure 5-22.

6. Release the mouse when you have reached the appropriate size rectangle.

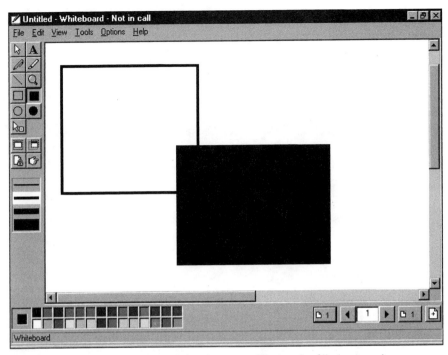

Figure 5-22   The Rectangle tool drawing an unfilled and a filled rectangle.

Follow these steps to draw a circle:

1. Click the Circle tool on the toolbar. Choose either the filled or unfilled circle.

2. Adjust the line width, as described earlier in this chapter.

3. Click a color from the color palette at the bottom of the document window, or use the color selector to create a custom color.

4. Move the cursor into the document window.

5. Click and hold while dragging the mouse, as shown in Figure 5-23.

6. Release the mouse when you have reached the appropriate size circle.

NOTE   Many drawing programs allow you to draw a perfect square and a perfect circle by holding the Shift key while you drag the mouse. Not so with the Whiteboard. You can get close, but no cigar!

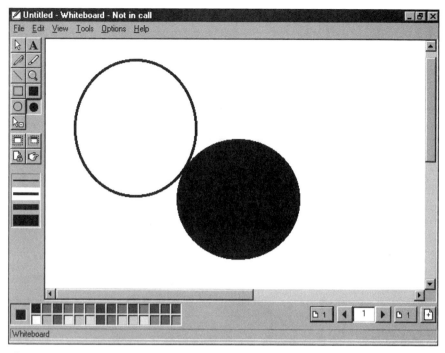

Figure 5-23   The Circle tool drawing an unfilled and a filled circle.

Highlighting

The Whiteboard gives you two ways to highlight an object:

* Highlight tool
* Remote Pointer

The Highlight tool functions much like a highlighter pen used to accent a paper book.

Follow these steps to accent an object with the Highlight:

1. Click the Highlight tool ![pen icon] on the toolbar.

2. Adjust the line width, as described earlier in this chapter.

3. Click a color from the color palette at the bottom of the document window, or use the color selector to create a custom color.

4. Move the cursor into the document window.

5. Click and hold while dragging the mouse, as shown in Figure 5-24.

6. Release the mouse when you have highlighted the appropriate section.

Figure 5-24 The Highlight tool accenting text with a transparent color.

Follow these steps to highlight an object with the Remote Pointer:

1. Click the Remote Pointer on the toolbar and the pointing hand appears in the document window.

2. Move the cursor into the document window.

3. Click and hold the hand while dragging the mouse, as shown in Figure 5-25.

4. Release the mouse when you have positioned the hand in the appropriate area.

5. To remove the Remote Pointer, click the icon once again.

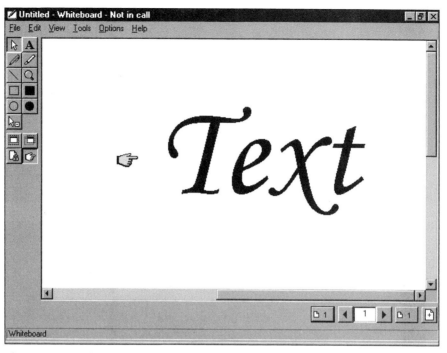

Figure 5-25 The Remote Pointer highlighting text.

Cutting and Pasting on the Whiteboard

The Whiteboard gives you the ability to paste anything on the clipboard into the document window including two advanced pasting options found on the toolbar:

* Select window
* Select area

Follow these steps to paste a window into the document:

1. Click the Select Window icon on the toolbar. The dialog box shown in Figure 5-26 appears.

Figure 5-26 The Whiteboard Select Window dialog box.

2. Click OK.

3. Click a window and it is pasted into the Whiteboard document window.

TIP The Select Window command is a great feature when you use NetMeeting as a distance learning medium. When you use this command, you can quickly paste any open window onto the Whiteboard — a very useful aid in answering questions.

Follow these steps to paste any area of the screen onto the Whiteboard:

1. Click the Select Area icon 🔲 on the toolbar. The dialog box shown in Figure 5-27 appears.

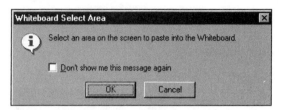

Figure 5-27 The Whiteboard Select Area dialog box.

2. Click OK.

3. Click and drag the mouse to marquee an area of the screen.

4. Release the mouse and the selection is pasted onto the Whiteboard.

Erasing the Whiteboard

Every so often you will probably make a mistake and need to erase something that you have created. If you are familiar with the Eraser feature in Microsoft Paint, pay close attention to this section because NetMeeting is completely different.

Follow these steps to erase an object from the Whiteboard:

1. Click the Select tool 🔖 on the toolbar.

2. Click the object that you want to erase, as shown in Figure 5-28.

3. Choose **Edit** → **Delete** .

4. Press Control+Z if you erased in error and want the object to return.

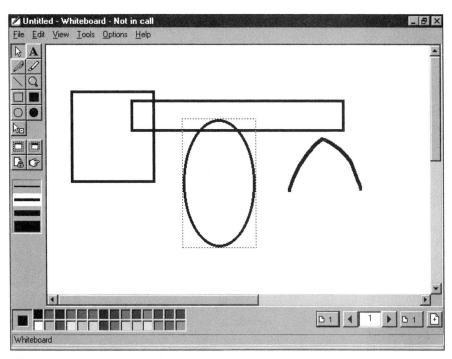

Figure 5-28   Selecting an object in preparation to erase it.

Follow these steps to erase all objects on a page:

1. Choose [Edit] → [Select All] from the menu bar to select every object in the document, as shown in Figure 5-29.

2. Choose [Edit] → [Delete] from the menu bar.

3. Press Control+Z if you erased in error and want all of the objects to return.

You can erase the entire page by choosing [Edit] → [Clear Page] from the menu bar. The Clears the current page dialog box appears just to make sure that you want to do it. If you click Yes, every object on the page will be cleared, but be warned. Using this method does not allow you to use the Control+Z command. Your items are gone forever!

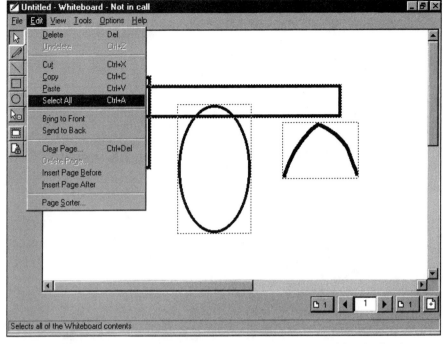

Figure 5-29 Choosing the Select All command to select every object in the document window.

Saving the Whiteboard

After working so hard to create such a beautiful Whiteboard document, it would be a shame to loose it all. NetMeeting gives you the ability to save your Whiteboard drawings.

To save the Whiteboard, follow these steps:

1. Choose **File** → **Save** from the menu bar. The Save As dialog box shown in Figure 5-30 appears.

2. Use the pop-up menu to choose the destination folder and enter a file name for the Whiteboard document, as shown in Figure 5-30.

3. Click Save.

Your Whiteboard drawing has been saved to the My Documents folder.

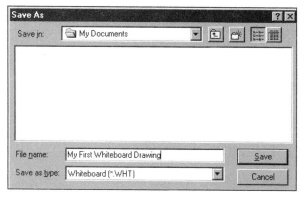

Figure 5-30 The Save As dialog box.

Opening a Whiteboard Document

After you have saved the Whiteboard, it's important to know how to retrieve it.

Follow these steps to open a Whiteboard document:

1. Choose File → Open from the menu bar. The Open dialog box shown in Figure 5-31 appears.

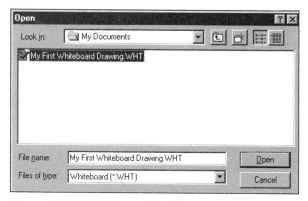

Figure 5-31 The Open dialog box.

2. Click on the Whiteboard document you want to open, as shown in Figure 5-31. In this example, the file is the Whiteboard saved from the previous section.

3. Click Open.

The saved Whiteboard opens and can be shared with each participant in the conference. The Whiteboard can also be edited and then resaved for future use.

TIP Create Whiteboard documents prior to your NetMeeting conference. It will save you time and be less stressful, especially if you are not an accomplished artist. You can create a "home page," much like those found on the Internet to introduce yourself (see the "Bonus" section of this chapter). Remember, communicating in NetMeeting is different than traditional methods. The Home Page Whiteboard document can be used over and over again, helping you get your message communicated.

Speaking of communication, the next section teaches you how to use the Whiteboard feature during an actual conference.

Communicating on the Whiteboard

As mentioned earlier, the Whiteboard feature is unique to NetMeeting because it can be used without being in a live conference. You can create and save your Whiteboard documents to use later. But when it's time to put them to work, you'll need to know how to do it.

Follow these steps to use the Whiteboard feature in a conference:

1. Launch NetMeeting and connect to a ULS server, as described in Chapter 1.

2. Address and connect to a conference participant or participants, as described in Chapter 2.

3. Inform the remote participant(s) that you are going to use the Whiteboard.

4. Use one of the four methods described earlier in this chapter to select the Whiteboard feature. For now, press Control+W.

5. Arrange your workspace for the type of conference you are conducting.

TIP If you are using the Internet Phone to communicate, just leave the Whiteboard document window at maximum size. You probably won't need any other desktop space. If you are using Chat, arrange the Whiteboard window and Chat window so they overlap. This way you can toggle between the windows. If you are using the Video Conferencing feature, reduce both windows and place them either side by side or on top of one another. This way you can see both windows.

6. Click the Lock Contents icon if you don't want the other participants to edit the Whiteboard. For now, though, do not click the Lock Contents icon; you want all participants to have access to edit the document.

7. Use the drawing features to communicate your message.

8. Encourage the other participants to add to the drawing.

9. Choose **Edit** → **Copy** to copy items to the clipboard.

10. Choose **Edit** → **Paste** to paste items on the clipboard into the Whiteboard document window.

11. Click the Add Page button to add additional pages.

12. Click the Highlight tool to highlight text and graphics.

13. Click the Remote Pointer icon to emphasize your message.

14. Choose **File** → **Save** to save the Whiteboard document created in the conference.

15. Choose **File** → **Exit** to leave the Whiteboard feature.

BONUS

5

Creating a Whiteboard "Home Page"

If you stop and think, you can probably develop some great ideas for using the Whiteboard to benefit your business and personal life. You can create your own personal Whiteboard home page, or you can create a home page for your best friend.

By creating and saving the home page, you can use it in any NetMeeting conference to let the other participants get to know you or your best friend a little better. By using a few "off-the-shelf" graphic tools, you can do a pretty professional job as well.

Follow these steps to create a Whiteboard home page for Sierra the Wonder Dog:

1. Click the Whiteboard icon on the main toolbar.

2. Copy and paste a background from a clipart CD onto the Whiteboard, as shown in Figure 5-32.

Figure 5-32   Copying a background onto the Whiteboard from a clip art CD.

3. Click the Text Tool **A** and type **Sierra's Home Page**, as shown in Figure 5-33.

4. Copy and paste a picture of Sierra, or a reasonable facsimile, as shown in Figure 5-34.

5. Click the Rectangle tool and add a solid black rectangle. Then add a slightly smaller solid white rectangle on top, as shown in Figure 5-35.

6. Click the Text tool and add any personal information that you want to divulge, as shown in Figure 5-36.

7. Copy and paste one final element into the Personal Data section of the home page. As you can see from Figure 5-37, it should be extra special.

8. Choose **File** → **Save** from the menu bar and enter a filename.

9. Choose **File** → **Open** to open the home page whenever you're ready to share in a conference.

Figure 5-33 Adding a title to your home page.

Figure 5-34 Adding a personal picture.

Figure 5-35 Adding a white rectangle with a black border by overlaying two filled rectangles.

Figure 5-36 Adding personal information to the home page.

Figure 5-37 Adding the final touch.

Summary

This chapter covered the multifaceted Whiteboard. You learned how to select the Whiteboard feature, adjust the Whiteboard settings, and use the tools to create graphic communications. You even learned how to make a Whiteboard home page that can be used in a variety of ways.

Later chapters discuss even more effective uses of this feature, but for now, *practice*. The Whiteboard is not easy to master. Trying different things, making mistakes, and trying again is the only way to become a Whiteboard expert.

Next, you'll learn how to use the Chat feature. Even if you have audio and video capabilities, you need to understand Chat. So turn to the next chapter and start chatting.

CHAPTER SIX

CHATTING

IN THIS CHAPTER YOU LEARN THESE KEY SKILLS

I f you have ever logged onto a service such as America Online (AOL), you have probably been in a chat session. NetMeeting's Chat feature is probably the most familiar of all communication methods. So, if you are an experienced chatter, skim through this chapter to understand how to access the feature in NetMeeting, and then move on to Chapters 9 through 12 to put the Chat feature into practice. If you don't have experience in chatting, read this chapter very closely. You will use the Chat feature in almost every NetMeeting conference.

So, what is Chat? Chat is a text-based mechanism for communicating. Participants in the conference "talk" to each other using standard text messages. This may sound rather simple, but it takes a lot of work and patience to become proficient.

In this chapter, you learn the basics of Chat. In addition, you discover another chat product from Microsoft Chat. So dig in and begin chatting.

NOTE   For a preview of a few of the important features you'll find in this chapter, turn to the Discovery Center. You can use the page references in the Discovery Center to quickly find additional information.

Time for a Chat

To access most of NetMeeting's features, you must first be in a conference; but, this is not the case with Chat. You can launch Chat without being connected to your ULS.

Follow one of these four options to select Chat:

1. Choose [Tools] → [Chat] from the menu bar, as shown in Figure 6-1.

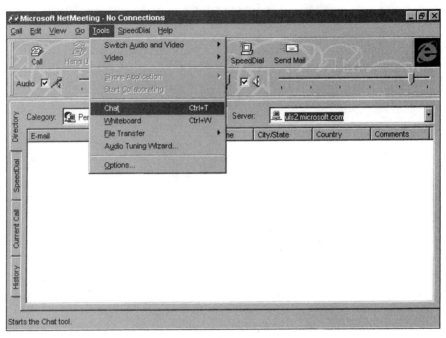

Figure 6-1 Selecting Chat from the menu bar.

2. Click the Chat button on the main toolbar, as shown in Figure 6-2.

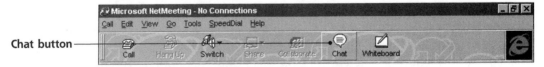

Chat button

Figure 6-2 Selecting Chat from the main toolbar.

3. Press Control+T.

4. Click the NetMeeting icon in the taskbar, if you have this feature activated in the General Preferences tab, and then click the Chat icon, as shown in Figure 6-3.

Figure 6-3 Selecting Chat from the taskbar.

Chatty Preferences

You must first locate the preferences before you can set them. The Chat preferences are not located with most of the other preferences in NetMeeting. To access the Chat setting, you must first select Chat in one of the four ways described in the previous section. After you have accomplished this, you will see the Chat window, as shown in Figure 6-4. From this window, you can adjust the two settings used in Chat:

* Fonts
* Chat Format

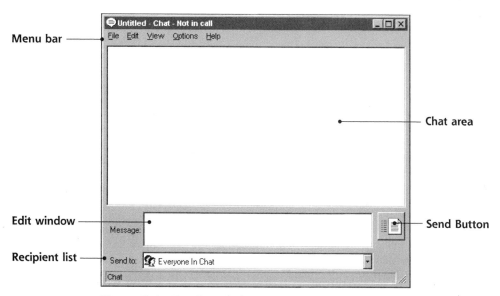

Figure 6-4 The Chat window.

Adjusting Fonts

Because Chat is text-based, you must be able to adjust the font attributes. Without this ability, you may not be able to read the text being entered — making Chat ineffective.

Follow these steps to adjust the Chat fonts:

1. Choose Options → Font from the menu bar and the Font dialog box shown in Figure 6-5 appears.

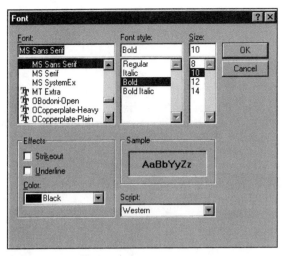

Figure 6-5   The Font dialog box.

2. Click the font, font style, size, effect, and color you want to display in the Chat window. An example of your selection is shown in the sample window.

3. Click OK to return to the Chat window.

TIP   Adjust the size of the text to fit comfortably in the Chat window. Because you can resize the window, it may be necessary to adjust the font size several times during a Chat session. You can change the font settings at any time, even during a conference.

TIP   Even though your computer is loaded with hundreds of fancy type styles, it is better to be plain and simple when you use Chat. The goal of a Chat session is to communicate, not be artistically creative. Figure 6-6 shows the results of using a creative font. Reading line after line of the Mistral font would be a problem. Choosing a font such as Helvetica (pronounced *Hel-vet-i-ca*), is not as creative but, as Figure 6-7 shows, it's easier on the eyes.

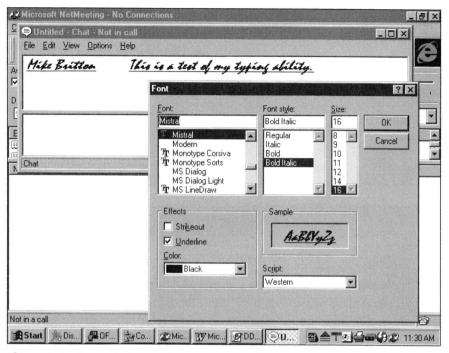

Figure 6-6 Using the Mistral font as your Chat font.

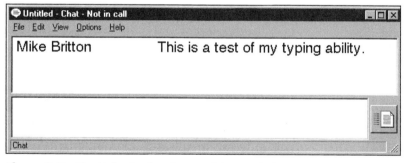

Figure 6-7 The Helvetica font is a much better choice.

Adjust the Format

Being able to see what you type and the response of other participants is essential in a Chat session. Without this ability, there is no communication. Chat allows you to customize the following items:

* Information displayed
* Format of the message

To adjust the information displayed, follow these steps:

1. Choose [Options] →[Chat Format] from the menu bar of the Chat window. The Chat Format dialog box appears, as shown in Figure 6-8.

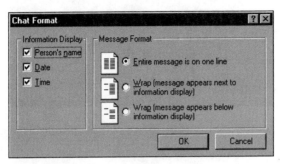

Figure 6-8 Chat Format dialog box.

2. Click Person's name to have your name and the other participants' names displayed, as shown in Figure 6-9.

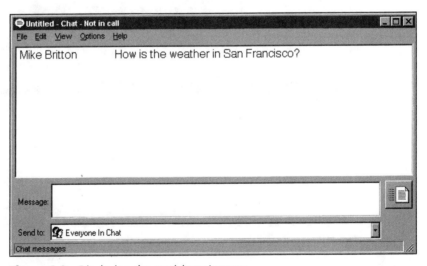

Figure 6-9 Displaying the participant's name.

 TIP Choose this option whenever you are in a Chat session. If you do not choose it, you do not have a clue who is typing. You can get yourself into some big trouble by responding to the wrong person.

3. Click Date to display the date of the message, as shown in Figure 6-10.

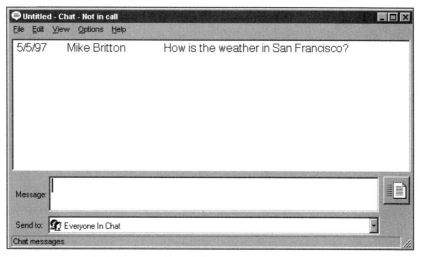

Figure 6-10   Displaying the date of the message.

4. Click Time to display the time of the message, as shown in Figure 6-11.

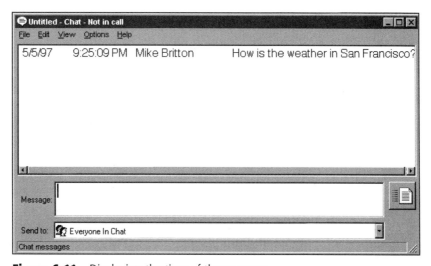

Figure 6-11   Displaying the time of the message.

To adjust the message format, follow these steps:

1. Choose   Options   → Chat Format   from the menu bar of the Chat window. The Chat Format dialog box appears. (Refer back to Figure 6-8.)

2. Click Entire message is on one line to display Chat messages on a single line.

TIP   **Choosing the single line option of Chat is not a good idea, especially if you have the date, time, and name options checked. (Refer back to**

Figure 6-11.) The message has moved out of the viewing window, and you must scroll to the right to read each message. This process is tedious, time consuming, and not much fun. To solve this problem, go to the next step.

3. Click Wrap (message appears next to information display) to wrap the message so it can be read. Figure 6-12 shows the same message with the Wrap option checked.

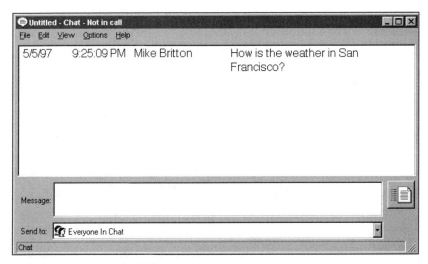

Figure 6-12 Using the Wrap (next to) option.

4. Click Wrap (message appears below information display) to wrap the message and have it appear below the date, time, and name. (See Figure 6-13 for an example.)

TIP Unless you have trouble remembering what time and date it is, or you have a business need to record the time and date of each message, don't use these options. The time and date repeated over and over again is very annoying. It is recommended to set only the Person's name and Wrap (next to) options. By doing so, you will always know who is talking and be able to read the text, even if the size of the window is changed, as shown in Figure 6-14.

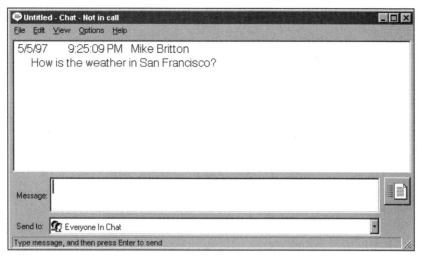

Figure 6-13 Using the Wrap (below) option.

Figure 6-14 Using the Person's name and Wrap (next to) options.

Just What Is Chat, Anyway?

As mentioned earlier, Chat is a text-based mechanism for communicating and it's important that you understand and become efficient using this feature. Even if you have audio and video capabilities, NetMeeting only supports these for the first two people in a conference. Each additional participant will need to use Chat or the Whiteboard to communicate. Because the Whiteboard is primarily a graphic-based communication method, Chat is the only good way for additional participants to join in.

Simultaneous Chatting

When one person in a conference chooses Chat, the Chat window appears on all computers. Everyone in the meeting can type messages simultaneously and see what others have entered. When under control, a Chat session can be very productive. When out of control, it's a nightmare. Later chapters will discuss how to apply the Chat feature in a productive way.

Freedom to Resize

When an application is shared in NetMeeting, the size of the shared window remains the same on all computers. For example, if someone minimizes the shared window, the window is minimized on everyone's screen. This is not the case with Chat. Each participant can resize, minimize, or maximize the Chat window independent of the other participants. This makes the Chat feature a more effective tool in a large conference and on different size monitors.

Audio Versus Chat

Chatting is much different than verbal methods of communication because there is no inflection and tone. A written word can be taken as hostile when it was meant to be funny. Therefore, you must watch what you say, or type, more closely than in audio mode. To further add to the problem, a Chat session moves very quickly and you must be a very good typist to keep up. Furthermore, Chat doesn't have a spell checker so if you are not good at spelling, it can be quite embarrassing.

 TIP Before you enter a Chat session in business mode, practice with a friend. Follow the steps described later in the "Conducting a Chat Session" section. Practice typing, and have a dictionary handy and learn how to quickly use it.

SIDE TRIP

SMILEYS AND ABBREVIATIONS

A sub-language has been invented to help solve the problem of tone and inflection when using Chat and to speed along the typing process. By placing Smileys and Abbreviations in your message, you can achieve emotions and you won't have to type as much. Listed here are some of the more popular Smileys and Abbreviations:

Smileys:

:-) or :)	happy face
:-(or :(	sad face
;-) or ;)	wink

Abbreviations:

Y	why
U	you
C	see
BRB	be right back
<g>	grin
<bg>	big grin
<vbg>	very big grin
BTW	by the way
CWYL	chat with you later
FWIW	for what it's worth
GIWIST	Gee I wish I'd said that
HHOK	ha ha only kidding
HTH	hope this helps
HTHBE	hope this has been enlightening
IMHO	in my humble opinion
IMNSHO	in my not so humble opinion
IOW	in other words
IRL	in real life
ITRW	in the real world
LOL	laughing out loud
OTP	on the phone
OTF	on the floor (laughing)
OIC	oh, I see
OTOH	on the other hand
POV	point of view
ROTFL	rolling on the floor laughing
TTFN	ta ta for now
TTYL	talk to you later
WRT	with regards to

6

Conducting a Chat Session

So far you've learned how to select Chat and set the preferences. Now it's time to enter into a live Chat session.

Follow these steps to use the Chat feature in a conference:

1. Launch NetMeeting and connect to a ULS server, as described in Chapter 1.

2. Address and connect to a conference participant or participants, as described in Chapter 2.

3. Inform the remote participant(s) that you are going to use the Chat feature.

4. Use one of the four methods described earlier in this chapter to select Chat. For now, press Control+T.

TIP An easy way to remember this keyboard command is to equate the letter *T* with *talk*. Whenever you want to chat, press Control+T and you're off and chatting.

5. Arrange your workspace for the type of conference you are conducting.

TIP If you are using the Internet Phone to communicate, maximize the Chat window. You probably won't need any other desktop space. If you are using the Whiteboard, arrange the Chat window and Whiteboard window so they overlap. This way you can toggle between the windows. If you are using the Video Conference feature, reduce both windows and place them either side by side or on top of one another. This way you can see both windows.

6. Enter your message into the Edit window, as shown in Figure 6-15.

7. Click the Send Message button to the right of the Edit window or press Enter. Your message is sent to each participant and displayed in the Chat area, as shown in Figure 6-16.

8. Wait for other participants to respond. Their replies appear in the Chat area, as shown in Figure 6-17.

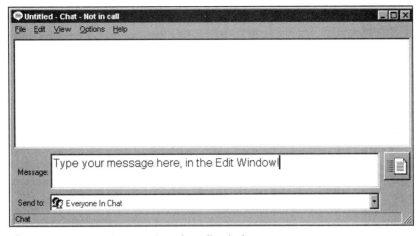

Figure 6-15   Entering text into the Edit window.

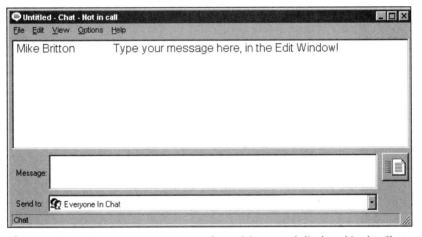

Figure 6-16   Your message sent to each participant and displayed in the Chat area.

   9. Enter a reply in the Edit window and press Enter. The reply appears on the Chat area, as shown in Figure 6-18. Use the pop-up window to send a message to just one participant.

   10. Continue the conference until you are ready to end the Chat.

   11. Choose **File** → **Save** to save the Chat session document created in the conference.

   12. Choose **File** → **Edit** to leave the Chat feature.

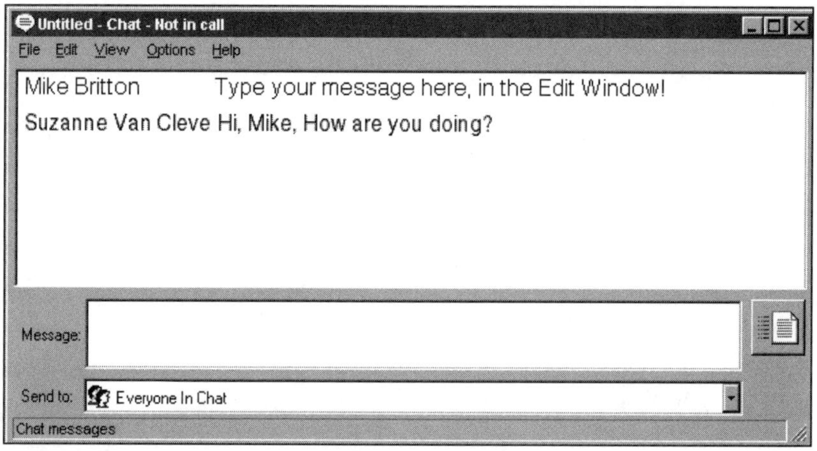

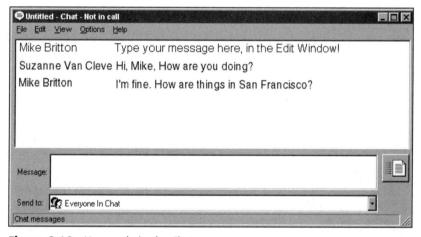

Figure 6-17 The reply from another participant.

Figure 6-18 Your reply in the Chat area.

BONUS

Microsoft's Chat Software

Using Smileys and Abbreviations can help you show your emotions when you're in a Chat session. Taking this one step further, Microsoft has developed a new Chat program named Microsoft Chat, which allows you to become a character in a Chat comic strip. It also enables you to graphically show emotion using an emotion wheel. Although this feature is not yet part of NetMeeting, it is a powerful tool for Chat communications.

NOTE At the time this book went to press Microsoft changed the name of the product originally called "Comic Chat" to "Microsoft Chat 2.0." You may therefore notice that some screen shots of the product reflect the original name. In addition, several enhancements have been made to the product, including integration with Net Meeting. See the Microsoft Web site for more details.

X-REF Microsoft Chat is included on the CD shipped with this book. You can find complete instructions for Microsoft Chat in Appendix C.

Your Microsoft Chat session begins when you launch the software and enter a chat room, as shown in Figure 6-19. You assume the identity of one of the comic strip characters; for example, your character is *Darth* in Figure 6-19.

Frame by frame the Microsoft Chat story develops. Figure 6-20 shows several new frames of the story starring *Lance* and several other characters.

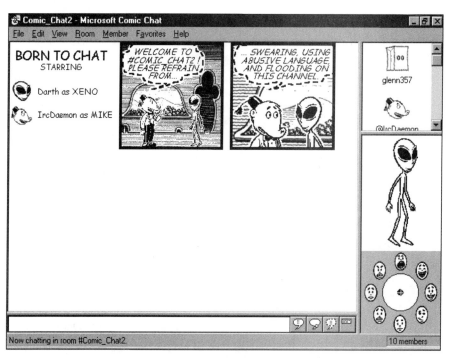

Figure 6-19   Entering a Microsoft Chat room as Darth, the alien.

Figure 6-20   The Microsoft Chat story develops.

To adjust the emotions of your character, you use the emotion wheel located in the lower-right corner of the Microsoft Chat window. Figure 6-21 shows the different emotions that can be created.

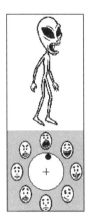

Figure 6-21   The emotion wheel.

As you enter text in the Edit window, your character appears in the comic strip displaying the emotion that you have set on the wheel. In Figure 6-22, Darth happily introduces himself to one of the participants.

Figure 6-22   Placing yourself in the comic strip.

As others respond, the comic strip changes and frames are added to display everyone's comments, as shown in Figure 6-23.

Figure 6-23   The story develops in Microsoft Chat.

Using Microsoft Chat can be fun as well as a good way to convey your message, and it makes a great counterpart to NetMeeting.

Summary

This chapter covered the basics of the Chat feature. You learned how to select Chat, adjust the preferences, and use Chat in a live conference.

Later chapters will teach you how to apply the Chat feature in your business and personal life and to combine this feature with the other features found in NetMeeting. For now, practice using Chat with a friend and become familiar with the Smileys and Abbreviations to speed along the conversation.

Next, you'll discover the wonderful world of video using NetMeeting's Video Conferencing feature. Lights, camera, go to the next chapter for Action.

CHAPTER SEVEN

VIDEO CONFERENCING

IN THIS CHAPTER YOU LEARN THESE KEY SKILLS

You might think that video conferencing is too high-tech and out of your league to be used. The hardware will cost too much and you won't be able to install it. Or, the cost of a video conference will break your bank account. Well, you couldn't be further from the truth. As with most technologies, the more sophisticated it is, the easier it is to install and use. Just think back to DOS and compare it to Windows 95. You needed a highly trained technician to add a piece of hardware in DOS. Using Windows 95, the software does everything for you but plug the device into the proper slot and Windows 99 will probably do that!

In fact, the Video Conferencing feature is probably the easiest feature of NetMeeting to understand, adjust, and use. The hardware cost is rather small and a video conference costs no more than a Chat session. You'll be amazed at just how simple it is. So comb your hair and smile because you'll be in pictures very soon.

NOTE   For a preview of a few of the important features you'll find in this chapter, turn to the Discovery Center. You can use the page references in the Discovery Center to quickly find additional information.

Hardware and Physical Requirements

Although NetMeeting has the Video Conferencing feature built right into the software, you do need the appropriate hardware to make it work. If you have been using the audio features of NetMeeting, you don't need anything further to hear or be heard in a video conference. However, you do need a camera to be seen.

Video Cameras

You have a wide range of options when selecting a video camera. You can choose between a black-and-white or color model, a camera with or without a built-in microphone, and a camera that simply plugs into the parallel port or one that requires you to add a board inside your computer. Table 7-1 compares four of the available options:

TABLE 7-1 Video Camera Comparison

Manufacturer	Model	Color / Black-and-White	Approximate Price
Vivitar	MPP-iI	Color	$220.00
Digital Vision, Inc.	DCVC	Color	$280.00
Connectix	Color QuickCam	Color	$220.00
Connectix	Grayscale QuickCam	Black-and-White	$99.00

Models, prices, quality, and performance are constantly changing. When you're ready to buy, do some research. Either log onto the Internet, read some trade journals, or thumb through a mail-order catalogue. Your video camera is just an overnight FedEx package away. Figure 7-1 shows the Connectix Color QuickCam.

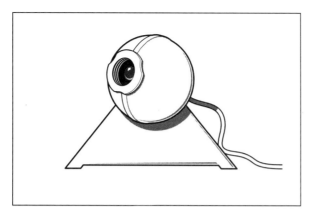

Figure 7-1 The Connectix Color QuickCam.

Unless you are a professional video producer or enjoy disassembling your computer, one of the parallel port video cameras will do just fine with NetMeeting. However, you probably have your printer currently plugged into that port. If this is the case, you have the following four options:

✳ Unplug the printer from the parallel port and plug in the video camera when needed.

✳ Buy an A/B parallel port switch-box.

✳ Buy an internal card to add another parallel port to your computer.

✳ Buy a parallel port pass-through device.

The camera manufacturers will tell you that adding another parallel port is simple. Although this is an accurate statement, you still need to open your computer, configure the new card, and adjust your system software. If you have never done anything like this before, you may not find it so simple. Be sure you know someone who has experience that can help you when your computer is in pieces and your system won't launch.

Space

The cameras listed in the previous section are primarily personal units. In other words, they set on or near your computer monitor and are designed to view one or two people. They do not have zoom capabilities or automatic focus, both requirements for conducting a video conference of a large number of people in one room. You can use these cameras to do just that; however, the results will not be very good.

The optimum distance between you and the camera is about two feet. This distance allows you to project an image of yourself that the remote viewers can easily see, and it allows for some background areas to be seen. This distance also enables you to better control the lighting. To maintain eye contact in the conference, the camera should be positioned on top of the monitor. Figure 7-2 shows the video image with the Connectix QuickCam two feet away and positioned on top of the monitor.

Figure 7-2   A properly positioned camera.

Lights

To get the best image, you must have adequate lighting. All other image adjustments of the camera depend on the presence of an adequate amount of light.

TIP   **If your lighting is such that you would use a flash with a normal 35mm camera, you need more light for the video camera to function properly.**

Figure 7-3 shows the result of inadequate lighting (left) and too much lighting (right). Be sure to compensate for the effects of fluorescent lights. Increase the Red level in an area with fluorescent lighting.

Figure 7-3   The results of inadequate lighting (left) and over exposure (right).

Setting the Video Preferences

You can find the Video preferences in the General NetMeeting Options window. To access this window, choose Options from the Tools menu on the menu bar. The NetMeeting Options window appears. The General tab is the default. Click the Video tab to access the video preferences, as shown in Figure 7-4.

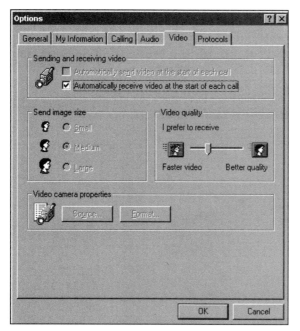

Figure 7-4 The Video preferences tab in the NetMeeting Options window.

To set the Video preferences, follow these steps:

1. Choose `Tools` → `Options` from the menu bar. The NetMeeting Options window appears.

2. Choose Automatically send video at the start of each call to send video when you launch NetMeeting.

3. Choose Automatically receive video at the start of each call to receive video from others when you launch NetMeeting.

If you choose the Automatically send video at the start of each call option, NetMeeting will automatically send video when you connect to a remote participant — that is, your picture will appear on the remote monitor. Although this feature will save you keystrokes, you must remember that the other participant can see you even if they don't have a video camera installed. So make sure you look nice and smile.

4. Choose one of the three image size options. For now, though, choose Medium.

TIP By choosing Large, you will see the size image shown in Figure 7-5. Choosing Medium will result in an image the size of Figure 7-6. The Small setting is shown in Figure 7-7. The bigger the image you send, the slower the performance. Start with the Medium setting and adjust up or down from there based on the performance of your computer and your connection. Note that the images printed in this book will appear differently than they do on a monitor.

Figure 7-5   Large image size.

Figure 7-6   Medium image size.

Figure 7-7   Small image size.

5. Move the Video quality slider to the left (Low) to increase the video compression. The motion will be faster but the image quality will be lower, as shown in Figure 7-8.

Figure 7-8 Video quality slider set to Low.

6. Move the Video quality slider to the right (High) to decrease the video compression. The motion will be slower but the quality will be higher, as shown in Figure 7-9.

Figure 7-9 Video quality slider set to High.

7. Click the Source button to access the Camera Adjustments dialog box. The settings shown in Figure 7-10 are for a Connectix QuickCam. The adjustments for your camera will vary according to the manufacturer.

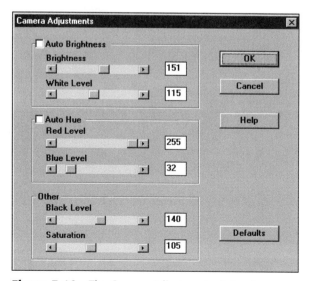

Figure 7-10 The Camera Adjustments dialog box.

8. Adjust the setting for Brightness, Hue, Black Level, and Saturation by moving the sliders, or click Auto Brightness and Auto Hue to have the camera make these adjustments automatically. See the manual that shipped with your camera for complete instructions.

9. Click OK in the Camera Adjustments dialog box. The NetMeeting Options window appears.

10. Click OK on the Video tab to complete setting the video preferences.

Selecting the Video Feature

I f you chose not to select the Automatically send video option described previously, you will need to launch the video window manually. Remember that the My Video window must be open on your computer for video to be sent to remote participants.

To manually select the Video Conferencing feature of NetMeeting, follow these steps:

1. Choose Tools → Video → Send . The My Video window appears, as shown in Figure 7-11. To simply preview your image, click the Not Sending/Preview button at the bottom of the window.

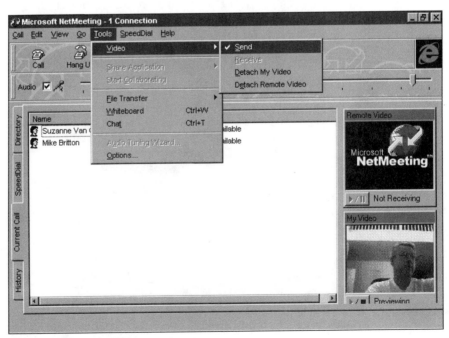

Figure 7-11 Choosing the Send Video command.

2. Choose `Tools` → `Video` → `Receive` from the menu bar to view the remote participant in a video conference. This option is not accessible if the remote participant does not have video capabilities.

Understanding Video Conferencing

NetMeeting video support delivers a high-quality video image over low-bandwidth network connections. In other words, you can send and receive good-quality video images by using the NetMeeting software over your telephone line. Before this type of support was introduced, video conferencing was accomplished by using highly sophisticated equipment, high-speed T-1 or faster lines, and by spending a lot of money. A typical video conference could cost at least $400 per hour.

NetMeeting works with any video capture card or camera that supports Video for Windows. It is also compatible with other third-party video conferencing software such as the Intel Internet Video Phone.

You can send video using your 28.8 Kbps modem over your existing phone line, you can upgrade to an ISDN connection, or you can send video over your local area network (LAN). This feature makes NetMeeting a great tool for intranets.

NetMeeting allows you to receive video even if you don't have video hardware. You can see the sender and use the audio capabilities to communicate or combine the video with Chat or any other NetMeeting feature.

You can copy your video images to the clipboard and then paste them into other applications or NetMeeting features, such as the Whiteboard. See the "Bonus" section of this chapter for detailed instructions.

Conducting a Video Session

So far you've learned how to select the Video Conferencing feature and set the preferences, including adjusting the camera settings. Now it's time to make a video conference connection.

To conduct a video conference session, follow these steps:

1. Launch NetMeeting and connect to a ULS server, as described in Chapter 1.

2. Address and connect to a conference participant, as described in Chapter 2.

3. Choose `Tools` → `Video` → `Send` from the menu bar. If you do not have the automatic option selected, the dialog box shown in Figure 7-12 will appear.

Figure 7-12 The NetMeeting Video dialog box.

4. Choose `Tools` → `Video` → `Receive` from the menu bar to view the remote participant in a video conference, as shown in Figure 7-13.

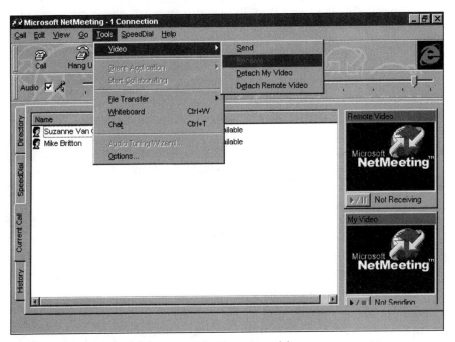

Figure 7-13 Choose Receive to see the remote participant.

5. Conduct your video conference using Audio, Chat, Whiteboard, or any other NetMeeting feature.

6. Click the Hang Up button from the main toolbar to end the conference.

7. Click the Close box in the upper-right corner of the My Video window, as shown in Figure 7-14, to close your video window.

Close box

Figure 7-14 Closing the My
Video window.

8. Click OK in the Close Video dialog box (shown in Figure 7-15) and your
   video window closes.

Figure 7-15 The Close Video dialog box.

BONUS

Copying and Zooming a Video Window

Y ou may have an occasion when you want to save a copy of a video image
and paste it into another application or onto the Whiteboard in
NetMeeting. You will also find it useful to zoom into a video window to
take a closer look at a subject. You can perform both of these actions right within
the My Video or Other Person Video window.

Copying a Video Image

When you copy a video image to the clipboard, the image becomes available to
be pasted into almost any application including the Whiteboard in NetMeeting.

To copy a video image to the Whiteboard, follow these steps:

1. Right-click on the My Video or Other Person Video window. A floating menu appears, as shown in Figure 7-16.

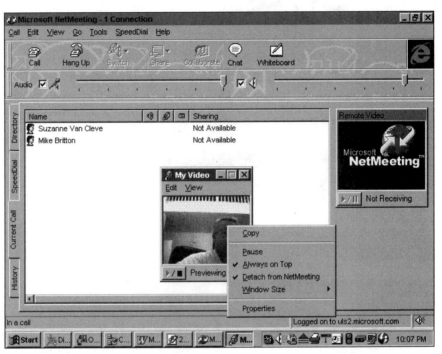

Figure 7-16 Right-click the video window to display the floating menu.

2. Choose [Copy] and the video frame is copied to the clipboard.

3. Click the Whiteboard button on the main toolbar.

4. Choose [Edit] → [Paste] from the Whiteboard menu bar and the video image is pasted onto the Whiteboard, as shown in Figure 7-17.

5. Modify the image on the Whiteboard using the tools described in Chapter 5. See Figure 7-18 for an example of adding a name to the video image.

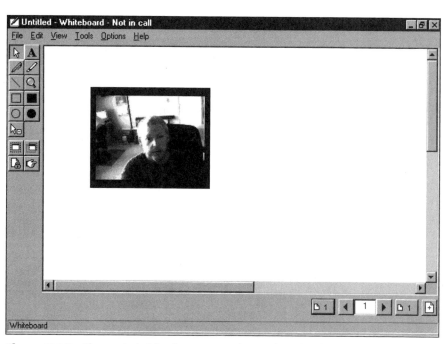

Figure 7-17   The copied video image pasted onto the Whiteboard.

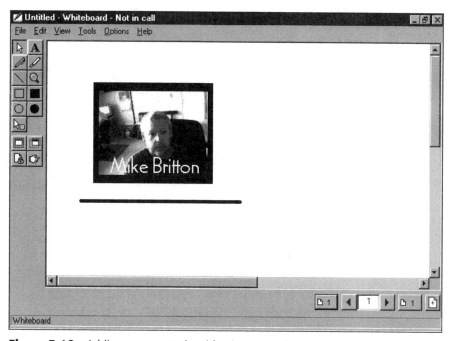

Figure 7-18   Adding a name to the video image on the Whiteboard.

Zooming a video image

By zooming into a video image, you can take a closer look at a subject. Although the resolution begins to deteriorate, as shown in Figure 7-19, this can still be a very useful tool.

To copy a video image to the Whiteboard, follow these steps:

1. Right-click the video window. A floating menu appears.

2. Choose Window Size and the size menu appears.

3. Click 200%, 300%, or 400% to double, triple, or quadruple the size of the window. For now, though, click 300% to triple the size, as shown in Figure 7-19.

Figure 7-19 The video image tripled in size with the original size shown in the upper-left corner.

4. Right-click the enlarged video window. A floating menu reappears.

5. Choose Window Size and the size menu appears.

6. Click 100% to return to the original size.

Summary

This chapter covered the basics of NetMeeting's Video Conferencing feature. You learned how to select the feature, adjust the settings of the software and the camera, and you discovered how to conduct a video conference. In addition, you learned how to copy and paste a video image into another application and how to zoom into a video image.

By now you have discovered all the audio, video, and data features of NetMeeting. The next chapter teaches you how to find someone to talk to, and how to list yourself on the User Location Service Directory so others can find you.

PART TWO

COLLABORATING WITH NETMEETING

THIS PART CONTAINS THE FOLLOWING CHAPTERS

CHAPTER **8** USER LOCATION SERVICE DIRECTORY (ULS)

CHAPTER **9** VIRTUAL MEETINGS

CHAPTER **10** CUSTOMER SERVICE AND TECHNICAL SUPPORT

CHAPTER **11** TELECOMMUTING

CHAPTER **12** DISTANCE LEARNING

After you understand the software, you need to put it into practice. In Part Two, you discover how best to use the features that you learned about in Part One. Here you get advice and techniques on how to run a virtual meeting and how to implement virtual customer service and technical support groups. Did you ever dream about working at home? Chapter 11 contains useful information on telecommuting, including what you'll need, how to get started, and how NetMeeting can make your dream a reality. How about taking a course without being in a traditional classroom? Chapter 12 is dedicated to learning from a distance. Anything is possible with NetMeeting.

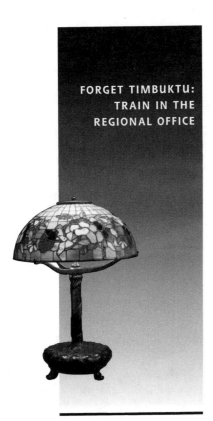

At PrintRite Printing Company, new sales and customer service reps are required to participate in extensive training and orientation sessions before they take on real accounts. The process once included a three-week training camp at the company's corporate headquarters in a remote part of the country.

Before the training program, participants were provided with a huge three-ring binder filled with procedures and policies, product information, and company data. Most of the materials needed updating, which meant that reps received paper-based updates and had to swap the pages in the binder. As a result of the page shuffling, the index usually became outdated, and overloaded reps quickly became frustrated with the reference material. (Not to mention the cost of copying and sending all those pages in the mail.) This process was repeated over and over and over again.

Thanks to a test program for reps that includes Microsoft NetMeeting, trainees now do a lot of their preliminary learning online, which reduces their training session in "Timbuktu" to one week at their regional offices, and forces them to become familiar with the company's technology base. The instructor starts with a comprehensive course outline that he e-mails to all prospective participants as an Adobe Acrobat .PDF file, along with instructions for downloading the Acrobat program. The instructor holds "classes" online once a week for a six-week period. Trainees log in directly from their desktop computers. They can also participate at any time in chat forums. "By eliminating the travel time and the anxiety of the typical classroom setting, the desktop conference allows us to be more productive and focus our time on what matters," says Ralph, one of the participants.

The huge binder has also been replaced with Adobe Acrobat files. Documents, available only in paper format are scanned, while spreadsheets and database files are converted directly to Acrobat files for easy access. Files are forwarded immediately to all participants during the training sessions so the guidebook is always current.

After the trainees complete their online course, they pack their bags once more and head to the corporate headquarters — but only for one week, as opposed to three. When they arrive, they've already covered the basics, and the technology of desktop conferencing makes them feel as if they already know each other, even though they've never met face to face. Much of the up-front work has already been done and they can get down to business in a much more productive manner.

USER LOCATION SERVICE DIRECTORY (ULS)

IN THIS CHAPTER YOU LEARN THESE KEY SKILLS

The Microsoft User Location Server (ULS) is used in conjunction with NetMeeting to find other users with whom they can conference. The server provides a dynamic directory of users that are currently running NetMeeting. Users can be accessed directly from within NetMeeting or from a Web page. In addition, you can create your own ULS server.

This chapter covers the basics of the User Location Service directory. By no means is this chapter a technical discussion of the server; that's another book. However, you will understand the importance of the ULS and how to select, update, and change your connection. So read on to discover the ULS directory.

NOTE For a preview of a few of the important features you'll find in this chapter, turn to the Discovery Center. You can use the page references in the Discovery Center to quickly find additional information.

Setting the Preferences

Before you begin to use NetMeeting, you must adjust the Directory preferences and choose a User Location Service directory. This next section shows you how.

Finding the ULS Preference Window

You can find the Directory preferences in the NetMeeting Options window under the Calling tab, as shown in Figure 8-1. From this tab, you set directory server information.

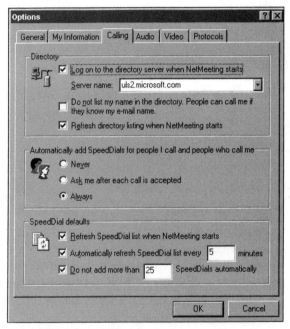

Figure 8-1 The Calling preferences tab from the NetMeeting Options window.

To access the Directory preferences, follow these steps:

1. Choose Tools → Options from the menu bar. The NetMeeting Options window appears.

2. Click the Calling tab to access the Directory preferences.

Setting the Appropriate Options

In this section, you select the directory server where your name and e-mail address will reside.

To set the directory server information, follow these steps:

1. Click Log on to the directory server when NetMeeting starts to automatically connect to your specified ULS.

2. Click the Server name pop-up window to select the ULS server in which you want to be listed, as shown in Figure 8-2.

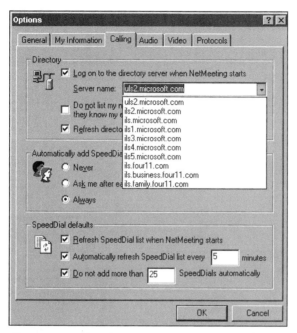

Figure 8-2   Choosing a ULS server to list your directory server information.

3. Click Do not list my name in the directory if you want to be unlisted in the directory.

4. Click OK to finish setting the preferences.

Selecting a ULS

After setting the preferences, you are ready to select and connect to a ULS. There is no hidden meaning or special function between one ULS and another. Microsoft directory servers that appear in the pop-up window simply go in order from 0 to 5, and one is no better than another. If you chose the Log on to the directory server when NetMeeting starts option as described in the previous section, you are already connected to the ULS you set in the preferences and your name will appear in that directory indicating that you are online. If not, your NetMeeting window will look like Figure 8-3 — no directory and no connections.

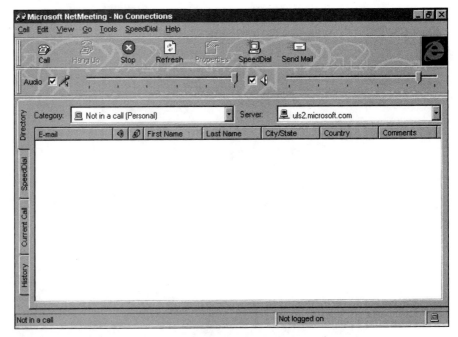

Figure 8-3 The NetMeeting window without a ULS connection.

To connect to a ULS, follow these steps:

1. Click the Directory pop-up window in the main NetMeeting window, as shown in Figure 8-4.

2. Click the ULS server to which you want to connect. NetMeeting automatically connects you to that directory server.

3. The dynamic ULS directory appears in the Directory window. If you chose your ULS, you will find your name among those in the directory, as shown in Figure 8-5.

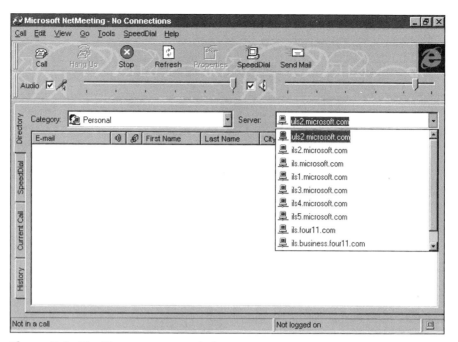

Figure 8-4   The Directory pop-up window.

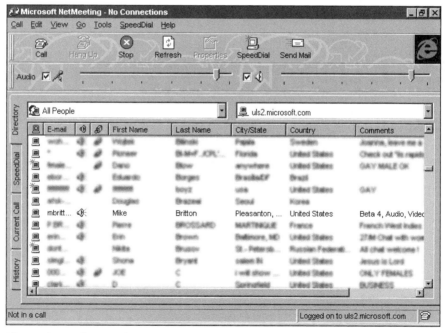

Figure 8-5   The ULS directory.

When setting the preferences, you probably chose the Log on to the directory server when NetMeeting starts option. If so, you are now connected to your ULS, but you can change the ULS server at any time during your NetMeeting session.

To change the ULS directory, follow these steps.

1. Click the Directory pop-up window in the main NetMeeting window, as shown in Figure 8-6.

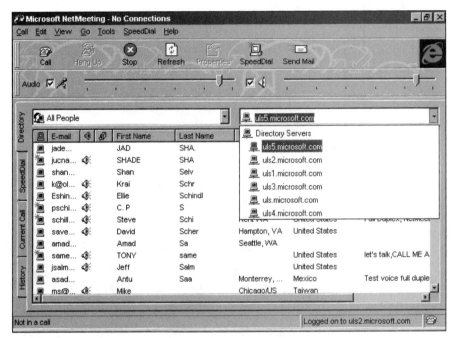

Figure 8-6 The Directory pop-up window.

2. Click the ULS server to which you want to connect. NetMeeting automatically connects you to that directory server.

3. The dynamic ULS directory of the new servers appears in the Directory window, as shown in Figure 8-7.

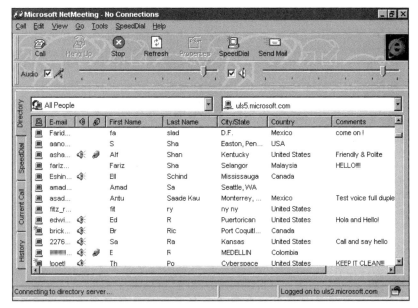

Figure 8-7 The new ULS directory.

Understanding ULS

The NetMeeting User Location Service provides a dynamic mechanism for NetMeeting users to locate other users on the Internet or corporate intranet. To accomplish this search, the ULS uses your IP address. Just as your unique telephone number differentiates you from all the other telephone numbers in the world and is needed for someone to call you, your IP address is needed to connect you to another computer. However, there is a problem. Many Internet service providers assign a dynamic IP address to your computer each time you connect to the service. Imagine having a different telephone number every time you made a call. Well, that's what happens with a dynamic IP address.

NetMeeting solves this problem by maintaining a real-time database of user information along with the IP address that is active when NetMeeting is first launched. It transparently connects two or more computers in a conference. You don't have to know any technical information.

Because the database is dynamic, it constantly changes. However, when you select and connect to a ULS directory as described earlier, it downloads the database as it exists at that time. Any future additions or deletions from the database do not automatically change in your Directory window.

Because the Directory window does not automatically change when the dynamic database changes, by nature it is constantly out-of-date. You are always looking at information that is wrong. To solve this problem, read the sections on updating and customizing the ULS directory.

Updating the ULS Directory

U pdating the ULS directory is very important. Unless you do this, you may be trying to call someone that is no longer running NetMeeting.

To update the ULS directory, follow these steps:

1. Click the Directory Refresh button located to the left of the ULS directory pop-up menu, as shown in Figure 8-8.

Figure 8-8 The Directory Refresh and Stop buttons.

2. NetMeeting automatically updates the ULS directory to which you are currently connected. Figure 8-9 shows the result of the update. Note that several people have left the ULS directory and several have been added.

3. Click the Stop button located to the left of the Directory Refresh button to stop the update (refer to Figure 8-8).

 NOTE You can follow the procedure for changing a ULS directory to perform an update as well. Simply click the ULS Directory pop-up window and choose the current ULS directory. This step will accomplish the same thing as pressing the Directory Refresh button.

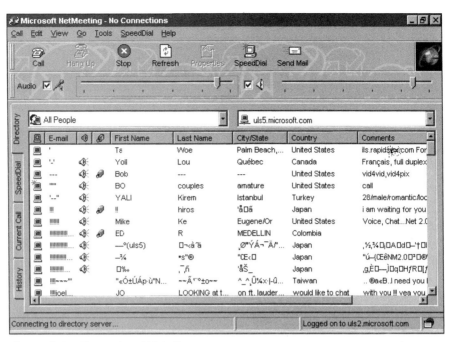

Figure 8-9 The updated ULS directory.

Customizing the ULS Directory

NetMeeting allows you to customize the ULS Directory window to suit your preferences. You can change the size of the information fields and alphabetically sort the information in each field. This feature is very useful because the ULS directory downloads in no logical order. Imagine trying to find a name in the telephone book if it wasn't in alphabetical order. It would be almost impossible. The same goes for the ULS directory.

To change the size of the fields in the ULS Directory window, follow these steps:

1. Move the cursor to the field names in the ULS Directory window.

2. Click and hold one of the dividing lines. The cursor changes to indicate that you can adjust the size of the field, as shown in Figure 8-10.

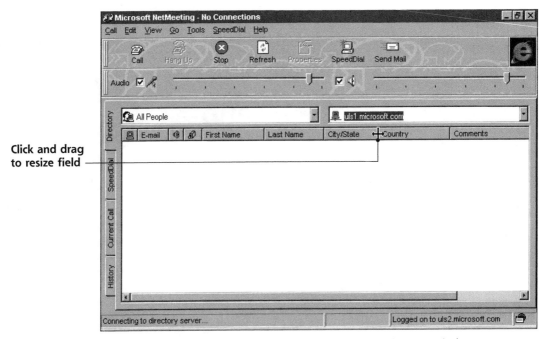

Click and drag to resize field

Figure 8-10 Changing the size of the fields in the ULS Directory window.

3. Move the cursor to the right to increase the size of the field, and to the left to decrease the size of the field.

TIP **To eliminate a field, follow the instructions listed earlier in this section but move the cursor until it covers the dividing line immediately to the left. This collapses that field and removes it from the window.**

To return the collapsed field, position the cursor on the dividing line of the collapsed field. The cursor changes into two vertical lines. Click and drag to the right. The field reappears.

To sort a field alphabetically, follow these steps:

1. Position the cursor on the name of the field in the ULS Directory window that you want to sort.

2. Click the field name.

3. NetMeeting will sort the field in alphabetical order from A to Z.

4. Click the field name again and the field will be sorted from Z to A.

BONUS

Establishing an International Connection

One of the major strengths of NetMeeting is its international communications ability. If you are on the upper-west side of New York City, it is as easy to connect to someone in Japan as it is to connect to another NetMeeting user in Manhattan.

To make the international connection, follow these steps:

1. Click the Directory pop-up window in the main NetMeeting window.

2. Click the ULS server to which you want to connect. NetMeeting automatically connects you to that directory server.

3. The dynamic ULS directory appears in the Directory window.

4. Position the cursor on the Country field in the ULS Directory window.

5. Click the field name.

6. NetMeeting sorts the field in alphabetical order from A to Z.

7. Scroll down the list to view the users from different countries, as shown in Figure 8-11.

8. Double-click the name of an international user.

9. Follow the steps in conducting a NetMeeting conference, as described earlier in this book.

TIP **Most international users communicate in their native language. To determine whether you are going to have a problem communicating, read the Comments field in the ULS directory. If you can understand what's written in the Comments field, you will probably be able to carry on a NetMeeting conference. If you can't (refer to the Japan section of Figure 8-11), you may need to review the Whiteboard because you'll need to draw pictures to get your message across.**

8

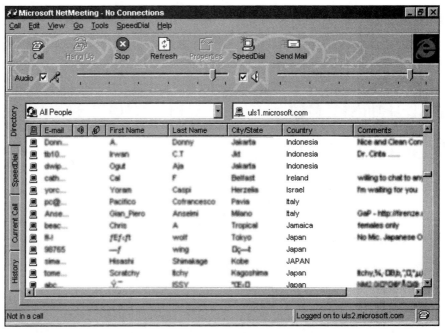

Figure 8-11 The ULS directory sorted by country.

Summary

This chapter covered the basics of the User Location Service directory. You learned what the ULS is all about, and you learned how to set the preferences and select a server to which you want to connect.

It is possible for you or your organization to have your own ULS server, which is preferable only if you are serious about using NetMeeting in a business sense. You can obtain details on setting up your own server from Microsoft.

WEB PATH Visit the following Microsoft Web site to obtain more information on setting up your own ULS server:

`http://www.microsoft.com`

By now you have discovered all the basics of NetMeeting. The next few chapters teach you how to apply these procedures in real life.

CHAPTER NINE

VIRTUAL MEETINGS

IN THIS CHAPTER YOU LEARN THESE KEY SKILLS

V irtual meetings have a George Jetson-ish ring to them, conjuring up images of your colleagues somewhere in outer space, phoning in for a chat. With NetMeeting, you can gather your team from all corners of the globe (outer space to come soon) relatively easily and with moderate expense.

Virtual meetings require a firm management approach to be effective; there's a lot of opportunity for one or two people to dominate the meeting while others try desperately to be heard or seen. This chapter provides a foundation for getting the most accomplished in your virtual meetings.

NOTE   For a preview of a few of the important features you'll find in this chapter, turn to the Discovery Center. You can use the page references in the Discovery Center to quickly find additional information.

Pros and Cons of a Virtual Meeting

Virtual meetings can dramatically change how people perceive meetings in your organization, and reactions are bound to be mixed. As the organizer, you'll need to be aware of the positive and negative aspects of virtual meetings.

Advantages of Virtual Meetings

Virtual meetings can be a terrific time and expense saver, because your attendees simply have to get to the computer or conference room nearby to join the meeting. That means they don't have to waste time commuting, and your Travel and Entertainment budgets will appreciate the eliminated cost.

Participants are close to any information they need because they're conferencing either right from their own computer, or at a nearby conference room accessible to their office. They can quickly call others into the meeting to answer questions or search for other information.

When you use the new technology tools, you can connect other participants from other locations at any time. You can share comments from virtually unlimited numbers of people through the Chat feature. You can show what you're talking about with the Whiteboard. And you can communicate even more effectively when your voice is complimented with video.

Potential Drawbacks of Virtual Meetings

You'll also need to consider the sacrifices you make when you're not face-to-face. Some people will have a hard time getting their ideas heard when they've got to break through the technical barriers as well as social ones. Many people are shy about public speaking, whether it's in front of 2 people or 20, and for some reason, putting them on a speakerphone or video camera magnifies their fear.

TIP **Get people on camera regularly until they become used to it. You'd be surprised how many video conferences are conducted looking at images of empty chairs or blank walls when people keep moving the camera so they won't be seen. If necessary, stop the meeting until they reposition their camera. Remind them that it's no different than being face-to-face, where everyone would see them anyway (Figure 9-1).**

Other folks will find a virtual meeting a good opportunity to hide, especially if it's a status meeting and they're not on schedule with their work. Others simply may not attend because they consider a virtual meeting to be less important than a "real" meeting. And, consider the effect of reducing business trips on the psyche of your attendees — many of them enjoy those monthly jaunts into the big city for a two-hour meeting and two days of play time. Still others simply hate technology and how it's changing their business lives.

As the meeting manager, you must instill the importance of the meeting in your attendees, and make it clear that it's the new way of operations. You can and should still have fun with video and the Whiteboard, but look out for the people with hidden agendas who may attempt to limit the effectiveness of your virtual meeting.

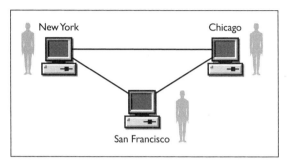

Figure 9-1   Virtual meetings can link participants in multiple cities.

Planning a Virtual Meeting

Planning a meeting can be a well-organized task if you focus on the basic questions: who, what, where, when, why, and how. Consider these elements:

* **Who #1:** Who's going to lead the meeting? This is the most critical role, and the meeting should be lead by someone who has both the authority and personality to run the show.

* **Who #2:** Who's going to participate? Smaller meetings are more effective than larger meetings, so invite only those who really have something valuable to contribute. Encourage your attendees to distribute meeting minutes to people they think should know what has been decided.

* **What:** What's the meeting for, anyway? Make sure you set an agenda (see the Side Trip "Establishing an Agenda" later in this chapter) and stick to it.

* **Where:** Where will each participant be located? You'll need to make sure that NetMeeting is properly installed and configured at each location. You can have multiple people in one location, as in a conference room, but remember that only one person will be running the computer. That means only one person at a time can actively participate in your meeting.

* **When:** Pick a time that's convenient for everyone. This is tricky when you're dealing with multiple time zones and your window of common opportunity can be very small. But, with virtual meetings, your associates in London can be connected from home in the evening, instead of keeping them in their office all night.

* **Why:** Set tangible goals for your meeting so everyone knows what they'll get for their time.

* **How:** Are you going to use the Chat feature? Use audio and/or video? Decide this ahead of time and again ensure that your participants have all the right tools, including microphones and digital video cameras.

SIDE TRIP

ESTABLISHING AN AGENDA

Setting an agenda is the most important part of meeting planning. If you carefully plan your agenda and allocate specific time periods for each discussion, you're likely to have an effective and productive meeting that everyone involved will appreciate. After all, we're "meeting happy" in corporate America today, for reasons none of us seem able to pinpoint. Think about meetings you've been in over the past week. How many of them did you consider valuable and productive? By creating an agenda, you'll focus your meeting for positive results.

To create an agenda, follow these steps:

1. Identify the goal(s) of the meeting. State this clearly for all participants.

2. Identify subjects to be discussed and indicate the key person for each. This person can be either the sole speaker, or the moderator of a group discussion.

3. Allocate a time for each subject.

4. Include logistical details: time, date, and location.

5. If it's the first virtual meeting, include technical matters as well: audio, video, Chat requirements, NetMeeting configuration, and so forth.

6. If the meeting will facilitate decisions that are significant to your organization, distribute the agenda to key personnel (that is, your boss) for feedback before routing to participants.

TIP   After you set an agenda, stick to it! Many meetings disintegrate into a waste of time when the agenda is ignored. You'll likely see the discussion moving in circles with no resolution or plan of action.

For tips on planning and running meetings, check out tips from the professional meeting planners at: http://www.mmaweb.com/meetings/. While their site is targeted toward people who plan large-scale meetings, their tips on setting agendas, scheduling, and running meetings are valuable for meetings of any size.

 TIP Use an electronic scheduling program to make your life easier. Such tools as Microsoft Schedule and Lotus Organizer are designed for workgroups. You pick a few times that are good for the meeting, and the application will search the schedules of all the participants. It's much easier than the endless loop of phone tag and the frustration of trying to manually match dates.

Notify Participants

After you have an agenda established, send it and any other pertinent documents to all participants. There's nothing worse than missing reports or documents that everyone should have read before the meeting.

Use e-mail to get your information out quickly. Attach your agenda and any necessary reports using a mail program that handles attachments, such as Microsoft Internet Mail, as shown in Figure 9-2. Use the Return Receipt feature if your e-mail supports it; it's useful to be able to track who received your message and who hasn't read it yet.

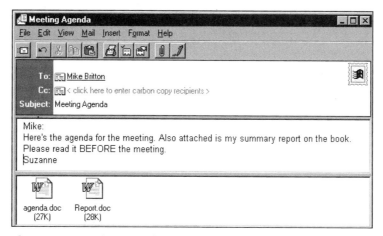

Figure 9-2 Sending e-mail with an agenda attached.

Finally, be sure to have all reports and documents handy during the meeting. With NetMeeting, you can use the Whiteboard to review visual elements, and you can use the Send File feature to immediately send files to anyone in the meeting.

Minutes or Action Items?

Should you designate someone to take and distribute minutes? That depends on your organization and the subject matter of the meeting. If it's a task force that needs to report on findings and accomplishments, documenting the meeting is a good way to keep everyone apprised of what's going on. If your meeting is limited to designated representatives from different parts of the company, documenting the meeting and posting the results for your organization may be useful. For small meetings among managers, minutes may be overkill and become "make work" for someone.

Instead of minutes, you can create a list of action items. Be sure to designate the following:

* A clear description of the task and deliverables if they exist. Deliverables can be a report, a recommendation, a prototype, and similar items.

* A key person responsible for the task. Make it clear that you will expect them to report back on the task at the NetMeeting conference.

* Other participants involved in the task. If they aren't present in the meeting, be sure they get an e-mail of the action items.

* Projected deadlines for the task, and/or milestones along the way. Milestones are clearly identifiable accomplishments along the way to completing a task.

Rules and Etiquette of a Virtual Meeting

Set the foundation for a good meeting by establishing some guidelines for how people can interact effectively. (In snobby circles, this is that thing called *etiquette*.) You can either send out guidelines before the meeting, positioning them as a primer for virtual meetings, or discuss them at the beginning of the meeting itself. It's probably a good idea to do both.

Follow these steps to be a good player in a virtual meeting:

1. Follow the moderator's directions for being recognized to speak, write, or draw. Remember that often everyone can't see and hear what's going on, and the moderator is responsible for getting everyone heard as efficiently as possible.

2. If you have a question, address it to someone specifically. That way you'll get one answer instead of several.

3. Be on time — better yet, be early. New technology can sometimes be a bit tricky to configure and it's courteous to respect the time of others in the meeting.

4. Pay attention. The days of doing your "homework" while sitting in a phone conference are over. There's a good chance you'll be using video now, or soon, so get used to focusing all your attention on the meeting and issues at hand. Imagine how much shorter meetings can be if everyone focuses on the discussion.

5. Stay put. It's really frustrating for the moderator and unfair to other participants if you wander in and out of the meeting, whether it's a Chat, audio, or video conference. Again, respect the time of others and it will be repaid to you in kind; otherwise, you could end up with virtual meeting chaos.

Conducting a Virtual Meeting

Now you're ready to conduct your first virtual meeting. Remember that it's a new experience for everyone, so lay the ground rules and encourage participants to follow them. Plan ahead and make sure NetMeeting is installed and properly configured before meeting day, especially if your meeting includes some higher-ups that you want to impress with your knowledge of this emerging technology. Set aside extra time to get everyone connected; if you have some real newbie users at various locations, try to identify the local technical expert and ask them to be available a half-hour before the meeting.

Connect the Participants

The first step in a virtual meeting is to connect all the participants and make sure that everyone is able to communicate. Otherwise, your meeting will not accomplish its intended purpose.

Follow these steps to connect the participants:

1. Click Start. You see the Start menu options.

2. Click the Programs command. You see the programs and the program folders you have set up on your system.

3. Locate Microsoft NetMeeting in the list of programs and folders.

4. After you have located NetMeeting, click it to launch the software.

5. A successful launch displays the NetMeeting splash screen.

6. If you are not already connected to your Internet Service Provider, a dialog box appears. Make sure that each window contains the correct and appropriate information for your account, and then click Connect. If you are already connected to your ISP when you launch NetMeeting, this dialog box does not appear.

7. Choose `Call` → `New Call` from the menu bar, or click the Call icon on the main toolbar. The New Call dialog box appears.

8. In the Address window, enter the identity of the computer you are calling.

9. In the Call using pop-up window, specify whether you are using a modem or a network connection along with the protocol you are using. For now, choose Automatic. (Refer to Appendix B for detailed information.)

10. Select Join the meeting named: if you want to call a conferencing service. In the option window, enter the name of the meeting you want to join in. For now, however, do not select this option.

11. Select This person is using PictureTel LiveShare if you know that the person you are calling is running PictureTel LiveShare software.

WEB PATH

LiveShare Plus data conferencing software from PictureTel allows you to easily share applications, files, and ideas over a modem or a LAN. Connecting to another LiveShare Plus or NetMeeting user, you can share multiple applications, even if only one person has the application. For more information, you can contact PictureTel Corporation at 100 Minuteman Drive, Andover, MA 01810. Or phone them at (508) 292-5000.

```
http://www.picturetel.com
```

12. Click Call.

13. An incoming dialog box appears on the computer of the person you are trying to call. The dialog box gives the recipient the option of accepting the call or ignoring the call. To answer your call, the person you are calling will click Accept.

14. When the person you are calling accepts the call, the Connection window will list you and the person you called. The status bar will show that the person you called has joined the conference. As others enter the conference, their names will be listed in the Connection window as well.

15. If you have trouble hearing or your voice is distorted, you can use the Audio toolbar to adjust the microphone and the speaker volume. Move

the sliders to the right to increase the volume. Move them to the left to decrease the volume.

16. After you have made all the necessary adjustments, you are ready to conduct your conversation. Talk into the microphone and listen through the speakers.

17. To connect another person to the conference, select a name from the Directory window and click Call from the main toolbar.

 NetMeeting supports meetings of up to 32 people. However, only the first two people connected with audio can participate in an audio or video call. All other participants must use a text or graphic feature to communicate.

18. When it's time to conclude your call, inform the participants in the conference that you are hanging up, and then click Hang Up from the main toolbar.

19. You are now ready to make another call or exit the program. To make another call, just follow the previous instructions. To exit the program, choose Call → Exit from the menu bar.

X-REF See Chapters 1 and 2 for complete details on connecting to participants and adjusting the NetMeeting settings.

Introduce the Participants

It's easy to introduce the participants, whether you're using a video conference or not. Remember that only the first two people in the conference have audio and video capabilities. If it's a large meeting, you can introduce people via the Chat feature by listing participants and some background on why they're participating (their department, divisions, job title, and so on). Or, if you want to show off your new digital camera or take screen shots using your video camera, you can introduce participants via the Whiteboard as shown in Figure 9-3. In any event, prepare these introductions ahead of time so you don't waste valuable meeting time.

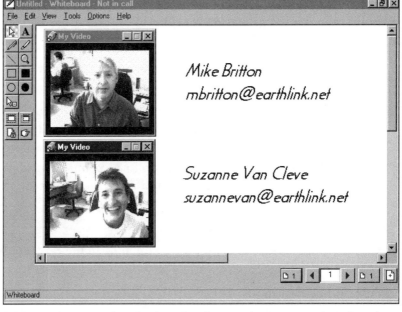

Figure 9-3 Using the Whiteboard and your video camera to introduce the participants.

Review the Agenda, Goals, and Time Frame

To immediately focus your meeting, put the agenda in front of everyone through the Chat feature, and ask them to review it as shown in Figure 9-4. Again, prepare and save this ahead of time. Make sure everyone is aware of time frames for each segment and for the end of the meeting. Participants will really appreciate it if you keep to schedule — everyone is busy and if you stick to your promises, people will come back to your meeting the next time around.

Reiterate the goals of the meeting, both at the beginning and the end. Make sure you've either achieved those goals or set alternate plans for resolving the matter.

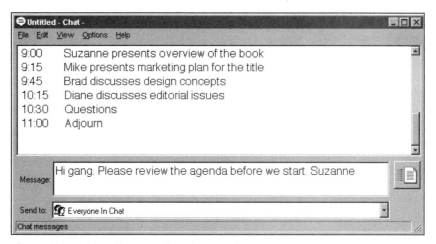

Figure 9-4   Using Chat to review the agenda.

Using the Chat Feature in a Meeting

Chat is the tool you will use most in a multi-person conference because only the first two participants have audio or video capabilities.

To select and use the Chat feature, follow these steps:

1. From the Current Call tab, click Chat on the main toolbar.

2. Arrange your workspace.

3. Enter your message into the Edit window.

4. Click the Send Message button to the right of the Edit window or press Enter. Your message will be sent to each participant and displayed in the Chat area. Use the pop-up menu to select a single participant. By doing this, your message will only appear in that person's Chat window.

5. Wait for other participants to respond. Their reply will appear in the Chat area.

6. Enter a reply in the Edit window and press Enter. The reply is sent to the participants.

 See Chapter 6 for complete details on using the Chat feature.

File Transferring During the Meeting

Transferring files is a great asset, especially when someone arrives to your meeting without the necessary reports or documents. Gone are the days of frantically trying to find fax machines located close to both the sender and recipient. You can send a file to all or any specific participant.

Follow these steps to send a file:

1. Inform the remote participant(s) that you are going to transfer a file.

2. Choose Tools → File Transfer → Send File from the menu bar.

3. Using the Windows directory hierarchy, choose a file to send by using the pop-up menu to navigate to the appropriate file.

4. Click the file you want to send, as shown in Figure 9-5.

5. Click Send. The file is sent to all the participants in the conference.

6. If the file transfer was successful, you will receive notification.

7. Click OK and the file transfer is complete.

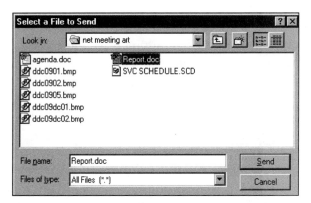

Figure 9-5 Selecting a file to send to all conference participants.

To send a file to only one participant, follow these steps:

1. Inform the remote participant that you are going to transfer a file.

2. Right-click the name of the participant in the Connection window to whom you want to send the file. A menu appears. Click Send File.

3. Using the Windows directory hierarchy, choose a file to send by using the pop-up menu to navigate to the appropriate file.

4. Click the file you want to send.

5. Click Send. The file is sent to only the participant you chose.

6. If the file transfer was successful, you will receive notification.

7. Click OK and the file transfer is complete.

9

Application Sharing During the Meeting

Sharing applications during a meeting is useful for viewing and discussing documents created in applications that all participants may not have. For example, let's say you want to show a slide presentation created in Persuasion, a book cover created in QuarkXPress, or a spreadsheet created in Lotus 1-2-3. Your participants only have the Microsoft Office suite and can't open these files themselves. Simply share the application in which you created the document and everyone can view the file.

To share an application in your virtual meeting, follow these steps:

1. Inform the remote participant that you are going to share an application.

2. Choose `Tools` →`Share Application` from the menu bar, or click the Share button in the Current Call tab window.

3. Highlight the application that you want to share and a dialog box appears. (Note that the application must first be running before it can be shared.) Click OK.

4. Click the application in the Windows status bar.

5. Click Collaborate in the main toolbar.

6. Arrange your desktop space so that you can access other NetMeeting features and controls.

7. Double-click in the Shared Application window to take control of the cursor.

8. Choose `Tools` →`Share Application` from the menu bar.

9. Click the application you want to stop sharing.

 See Chapter 3 for complete details on Application Sharing.

 TIP Use a common file format, such as Adobe Acrobat PDF, to share documents easily. If you can print a document and have the Acrobat software (or a conversion utility that supports .pdf), you can convert it into a .PDF file, which retains all the formatting and graphics of the original file. The Acrobat Reader software is available free from Adobe, so all your participants can download it and install it on their computers. It's a faster solution than sharing complex applications, and you won't have to worry about not having the right fonts.

 WEB PATH For more information about Adobe Acrobat, and to download the free Acrobat Reader software, visit Adobe at the following URL:

`http://www.adobe.com.`

Drawing During the Meeting

The Whiteboard feature is a handy tool for everyone to sketch their ideas, just like an old-fashioned meeting with flipcharts. The best part is that everyone immediately has a copy to keep, print, file, or edit at will.

You can copy and paste a chart onto the Whiteboard and use the Highlight tool and/or Remote Pointer, as shown in Figure 9-6, to emphasize a point. You can copy and paste a spreadsheet to review budgets, discuss artwork, review a contract, and so forth using this feature.

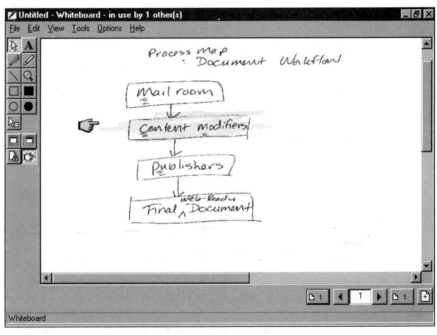

Figure 9-6   Using the Whiteboard Highlight tool to highlight a hand-drawn chart.

 Document collaboration is a capability within NetMeeting where you simply share the document and the application if needed. Any number of people in the meeting can make modifications to the file and see the results.

Take, for example, a budget. You can run "what if" scenarios by changing allocations or charge backs, increasing your sales figures, reducing your costs, and the like. That's useful information to see and analyze on the spot.

It's also useful as a teaching tool. You could create your budget templates for next year, and show all your line managers how you want them to fill in their projections.

But, imagine if two participants go head to head, modifying numbers against each other, such as budget allocations between departments. Technical and organizational chaos can result.

So document collaboration, while an effective tool used between two people, should be used carefully in a meeting setting.

 See Chapter 5 for complete details concerning the Whiteboard.

Wrapping Up the Meeting

When you're nearing the close of the meeting, take a few minutes to review the session and make sure everyone agrees on what transpired.

Follow these steps to close the meeting:

1. Review the accomplishments and note any important contributions and decisions made.

2. Set the next meeting. Do this while you have everyone together, with their datebooks, even if it's months until the next session. If it's a large group, it's even more important to plan way ahead of time.

3. Tell the group when minutes or action items will be available. If you've been keeping track of this online, you can simply use the File Transfer feature to everyone in the conference and be done with it.

DISCONNECTING THE PARTICIPANTS

After you have successfully conducted your virtual meeting, it's time to say goodbye and make sure that everyone is disconnected.

To disconnect the participants, follow these steps:

1. Notify the participants in the conference that you are hanging up, and then click Hang Up from the main toolbar.

2. You are now ready to make another call or exit the program. To make another call, just follow the previous instructions. To exit the program, choose [Call] → [Exit] from the menu bar.

Maximizing the Virtual Meeting Experience

If you plan carefully, and structure your meeting, you can help prevent organizational problems with your meeting. On the technical side, you should do a test drive before the actual meeting, especially if important people are attending. Every location has someone who's either a technical wizard or intrigued by computers: Seek out that person and make friends with him or her. Recognize that person's talents and thank him or her publicly. This person will help you out when you're in a crunch.

BONUS

From Paper to the Digital World

Still migrating from paper into the digital world? If you have important documents to share, but they're still trapped on paper, get an inexpensive personal scanner such as a Visioneer PaperPort. You can quickly scan in a document and paste it onto the Whiteboard. You can scan in receipts to justify that pricey expense report; resumes that have arrived on paper; diagrams; architectural drawings; ads; newspaper articles; business cards ... the list goes on. Figures 9-7 through 9-9 show samples of paper documents scanned into a PaperPort, saved as .BMP files, and pasted onto the Whiteboard.

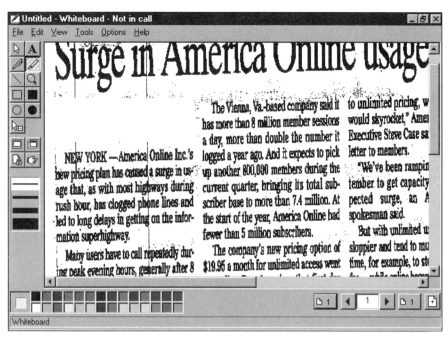

Figure 9-7 A newspaper image scanned with a PaperPort and pasted onto the Whiteboard.

Figure 9-8 A paper-based business card scanned with a PaperPort and pasted onto the Whiteboard.

Figure 9-9 A hand-drawn sketch scanned with a PaperPort and pasted onto the Whiteboard.

If you have a lot of paper to get digital, consider a larger scanner such as the Hewlett Packard ScanJet. You can make various adjustments to this scanner to enhance the quality and increase the size of your image, both of which will affect the clarity and transfer time of your image during the meeting.

TIP For detailed guidelines on managing paper in a digital world, see Tony McKinley's book *Paper to Web*, published by Adobe Press.

Summary

In this chapter, you learned how to plan your first virtual meeting. Setting an agenda, with topics and timing carefully thought out, provides a solid foundation for a successful virtual meeting.

You learned how to conduct a virtual meeting and how the interpersonal dynamics of a digital conference will vary a bit from the traditional face-to-face meeting. You also learned how to use audio and video in a meeting and how to integrate the Chat and Whiteboard features.

In the next chapter, you'll learn how to provide better customer service and technical support the virtual way.

CUSTOMER SERVICE AND TECHNICAL SUPPORT

IN THIS CHAPTER YOU LEARN THESE KEY SKILLS

This chapter discusses customer service and technical support. For purposes of this book, *customer service* is defined as the department that interfaces with your external customers, providing them information on products, sales, and technical problems. *Technical support* is defined as the internal department that maintains and supports the computer systems within your company. This department is also referred to as the *help desk* in many companies. No matter what you call them, customer service and technical support are two areas that represent picture windows into the inner workings of your company. Customer service is a window for the outside world to look in. In many cases, that window provides the only view a customer has of your company. Technical support is a window for the internal staff to look deep into the technical heart of the organization, often finding and curing problems before they happen. In many cases, these problems left undetected could cripple your organization.

It's ironic that these two vital functions of an organization are often the areas that get the least attention, funding, and support. They are often the most overworked, underpaid, and sport the highest turnover rate of any departments in your company. You would think that these picture windows would get polished daily. However, the truth of the matter is they often look like they haven't been cleaned in years.

To be fair, the technology tools have not been readily available to assist these departments. In addition, tools that are available are expensive, making it hard to establish a clear return on your investment. The good news is that NetMeeting has the ability to clean both of these windows and provide some clear solutions for customer service and technical support.

Combining NetMeeting with some of the sound principles described in this chapter will provide a return that will not only enhance your image with customers, but will keep your business functioning with minimal cost.

NOTE For a preview of a few of the important features you'll find in this chapter, turn to the Discovery Center. You can use the page references in the Discovery Center to quickly find additional information.

Planning for Virtual Customer Service and Technical Support

To have a great customer service and technical support solution, you must first plan and then implement. In this section, you'll discover how to plan; the following section explains how to implement. Read these sections very carefully. You won't find a lot of technical information or step-by-step instructions (see "How to Conduct Virtual Customer Service and Technical Support," later in this chapter, for this information). What you will find here is the foundation upon which the technical information should be built.

Assessing the Needs of Your Company

Every company is different and has different needs. Whether you have 5 employees or 5,000 employees, understanding your own organization is essential to establishing a great virtual customer service and technical support function.

You need to understand the following:

* Employees
* Customers

- ✳ Infrastructure
- ✳ Politics

EMPLOYEES

Needless to say, customer service and technical support are provided by employees. Assessing the workload/employee ratio is the first step in establishing good customer service and technical support. Finding the right balance between the workload and the number of staff members will result in employees who function well. An imbalance in this area will produce tired employees who have bad attitudes.

The second assessment is compensation. These employees are your eyes and ears to the outside world and to the inner workings of your organization. In many cases, the turnover rate is high due to low compensation accompanied with overwork and poor working conditions. Take a look at the compensation structure and the potential for advancement. Adjust the pay level to be commensurate with the value that these areas provide. You'll have happier employees who stay with you, even when the going gets tough.

The third assessment is training. Many companies just don't have time or don't make the effort to train employees. Evaluate the current level of technical expertise in your customer service and technical support staff. You may need to bring in consultants to do this, but it will be worth the expense.

CUSTOMERS

Understanding the needs of the customer is essential, not only in customer service, but in technical support. In the first instance, the customer is external. In the second, the customer resides within your organization. No matter how you look at it, they both are customers and both have needs.

Assessing the needs of your external customers will provide the basis for establishing the methods to serve them. Does your customer want to contact you by computer? If so, does your customer have the right hardware to audio or video conference?

Internally, you have more control. You can dictate that the customer contact technical support using the computer and that the internal customer has the right hardware. However, understanding the needs of the internal customer is just as important as understanding the needs of the external customer. What is the anticipated lag time between reporting a problem and receiving the service call? Is the internal customer comfortable using NetMeeting's new audio and video capabilities?

INFRASTRUCTURE

In the planning phase of a virtual customer service and technical support solution, you need to assess your current infrastructure. Don't underestimate the importance of this assessment. You can have the most highly trained employees, you can understand the needs of your customers, you can have all the latest hardware, and still fall flat because the wires connecting the computers or the servers storing the data aren't sufficient to carry the load. Look what happened to America Online in the first quarter of 1997. Their infrastructure was not capable of handling the load and many customers fled to other service providers.

The infrastructure of most companies is so poor that the cost to retrofit the organization becomes a financial nightmare. It's difficult for senior managers to part with thousands of dollars for wires and servers when the money could be spent to create new products or posted as profits. In many cases, management decides to implement new technology without updating the infrastructure. This is a recipe for disaster and never, ever works.

POLITICS

After you understand the needs of your employees and your customers, and you have examined the infrastructure of your organization, you need to take a close look at the politics within your company. Internal politics is usually something that isn't discussed. In many cases, it's ignored or even denied. But in every company, no matter how big or small, internal politics exist and causes problems if not understood and dealt with.

You need to assess who gains and who loses by implementing a virtual customer service and technical support solution. Understanding this information will allow you to deal with the situation before the new system fails.

Needs in a Nutshell

So to sum up this section, you need to consider the following when planning for good virtual customer service:

- ✳ Assess your employee/workload ratio
- ✳ Assess your employee compensation
- ✳ Assess the level of employee knowledge and training
- ✳ Understand the needs of your customer
- ✳ Assess your company's infrastructure
- ✳ Understand your company's politics

Implementing Virtual Customer Service and Technical Support

After you have planned for virtual customer service and technical support, you need to implement. To do this, you need to do the following:

* Establish your goals
* Map the process
* Determine what hardware and software you need
* Prepare a cost justification
* Obtain approval
* Purchase equipment and software
* Install computers and software
* Test
* Train
* Go live

Establish Your Goals

What do you want your new virtual customer service and technical support solution to accomplish? Do you want to provide a more personal interface with your external customer? Do you want to reduce the response time of a help desk call? Whatever needs you have discovered during your planning phase should be written down as goal statements and communicated with all those involved. By doing this, everyone will understand the purpose of the new system and it should help eliminate those nasty political issues that are sure to arise.

Map the Process

Yes, you really need to do this even though you think that it's a waste of time and effort. Map the current process and the proposed new process, and then compare. Look for redundancies and ways to simplify the process. Get as many people involved in creating the process map as you can and be sure to map the real current process. Figure 10-1 shows the beginnings of a typical process map.

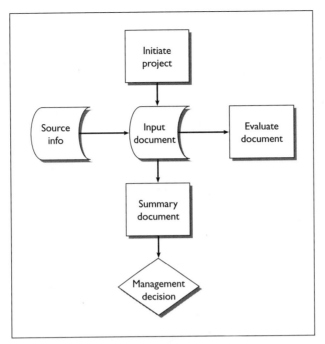

Figure 10-1 A typical process map.

 When one or two people map a current process, they may actually be mapping the process as they would like to see it or as they think it works, not how it actually works. By involving as many people as possible, you increase your chances of viewing the process as it exists. Understanding how a process actually works is vital in creating a new virtual process. If you want to be in FantasyLand, you'll need to go to Disney World.

 TIP There are many books on process mapping and many services available to help you accomplish this task. Use outside services. Not only will an outside service offer you an objective look at your process, it won't take as long to accomplish.

Determine What Hardware and Software You Need

Undoubtedly, you will need additional hardware and software to implement virtual customer service and technical support systems. Don't underestimate the cost involved. Even though NetMeeting is free, your computer requires additional hardware to audio and video conference. A simple sound card, microphone, and video camera could cost from $300 to over $1,000 per employee, depending on the quality level desired. In addition, there is a cost to install the hardware, test the new devices, and load associated software.

Prepare a Cost Justification

Unless your company has money growing on trees, you'll need to prepare a cost justification for your virtual customer service and technical support solution. Take into account hardware costs, additional software costs, time, and training. Don't forget there are also some "soft costs" that will occur, such as lost revenue during the training phase.

Obtain Approval

Prepare a concise, detailed report of the associated costs and the projected benefits. Even if you have a small two-person company and you're presenting this to your partner, do the report. Preparing this report will force you to think through the issues, look at the costs, and establish a benchmark for success.

TIP   Many companies have established approval mechanisms already in place. Most assume a level of Return On Investment (ROI) before any approval is given. Make sure you know what this level is, and don't overestimate the return of a virtual customer service and technical support system. If it doesn't make sense for your organization, don't implement it.

Purchase Equipment and Software

After all the approvals have been given and the signatures are on the dotted line, order your new computers and any additional software that is required.

TIP   Have your purchase order already written before obtaining approval and make sure that your computer supplier has all items in stock. By doing so, you'll assure a smooth installation. After receiving approval to implement, the last thing you need is a delay because a key device is backordered.

Install Computers and Software

Prepare a detailed installation plan. Keep in mind that when installing new equipment and software, the normal functions of a department can be reduced to zero. The excitement and anxiety level of the employees cannot be underestimated. During this time, very little "work" will be accomplished.

Test

Test, and test again before going live. Customer service and technical support have high profiles with both internal and external customers. Technology failures will happen, things will not be configured properly, and systems will crash. Keep this in mind and plan for the worst.

TIP **Install and test new systems during off hours. Use evenings, weekends, and holidays as time to install, test, and redo your virtual customer service and technical support solution. Never test with live customers; they may not continue to be customers if you do.**

Train

Everything you have planned and implemented is useless if those using the new system don't know how or what to do. Most companies do a terrible job in the training area. Plan for training and make sure that the cost has been included in the cost justification.

X-REF **You can use NetMeeting's features to do the training. See Chapter 12 for complete details on using NetMeeting to accomplish distance learning.**

In addition to training your employees, you need to train your customers. Develop an easy training mechanism to show your external customers how to take advantage of virtual customer service. You may need to do some marketing of this new service in addition to the training.

Go Live

After everything has been tested and everyone has been trained, it's time for you to go live with your virtual customer service and technical support solution. Determine the cutover date, inform both internal and external customers, and make the switch. Monitor the reaction of those involved and make adjustments as necessary.

To make the new system most efficient, you will need to gather data and analyze the results and then modify the process based on the results. In the next section, you'll discover the importance of data collection in a virtual customer service and technical support system.

Gathering and Evaluating Virtual Data

When you use a simple database program in conjunction with NetMeeting, you can gather data about your external customers, record technical problems of your employees, and provide an activity log that can be used to determine staffing levels.

Proprietary software exists that will do this for you; however, in many cases it's overkill and quite expensive. Unless you service thousands of customers or have thousands of employees, a simple off-the-shelf database program will do nicely.

Capturing the Data

Establish what data you want to capture during a virtual customer service call or a technical support call. Set up your database to efficiently house this information. Figure 10-2 shows the beginning of a simple database. When you use the Application Sharing feature, you can either enter the appropriate information and allow the customer to view it for accuracy, or you can collaborate and have the customer enter the information for you. Remember, the customer does not need to have the database software to collaborate. You can even use a proprietary software that only you possess and all of this can be accomplished while viewing each other on video and communicating through the Audio feature.

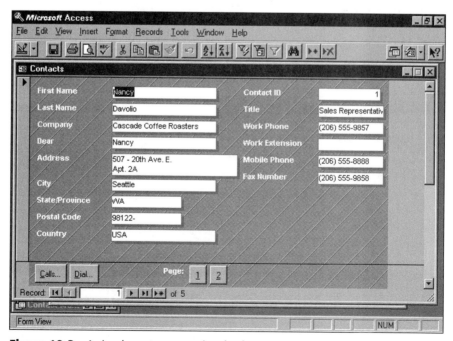

Figure 10-2 A simple customer service database.

Analyzing the Data

Capturing information for the sake of having it doesn't accomplish much. You need to have the ability to generate useful reports that add value to your company. Many proprietary systems generate reports that were specified during the creation of the system but don't allow for ad hoc reports. These legacy reports may have been useful when first created, but the growth of your business depends on analyzing current data with current needs in mind. Make sure that you have the ability to use the data you capture.

Conducting Virtual Customer Service

N ow you're ready to conduct a virtual customer service call. Remember that it's a new experience for everyone, so be patient.

The first step in a virtual customer service call is to connect the customer and make sure that you can communicate. Usually the customer will call you using NetMeeting, in which case you would simply answer the call. However, you may be in a situation where you need to call the customer.

Follow these steps to connect to your customer when you make a virtual customer service call:

1. Choose `Call` → `New Call` from the menu bar, or click the Call icon on the main toolbar. The New Call dialog box appears.

2. In the Address window, enter the identity of the customer you are calling.

3. Click Call.

4. An incoming dialog box appears on your customer's computer. The dialog box gives your customer the option of accepting the call or ignoring the call. To answer your call, the customer will click Accept.

5. When the customer accepts the call, the Connection window will list you and the customer. The status bar will show that the customer has joined the conference. If you have video capabilities, you will see yourself and your customer, as shown in Figure 10-3.

6. If you have trouble hearing or if your voice is distorted, you can use the Audio toolbar to adjust the microphone and the speaker volume. Move the sliders to the right to increase the volume; move them to the left to decrease the volume. You can also adjust the camera if the image is not adequate.

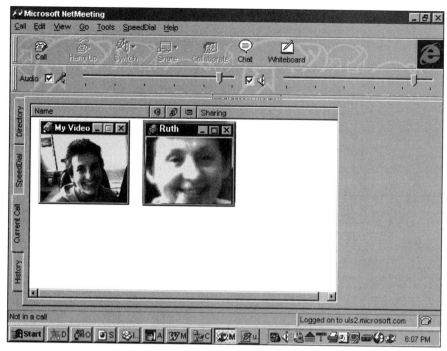

Figure 10-3 A video connection in a customer service call.

7. After you have made all the necessary adjustments, you are ready to conduct your customer service call. Talk into the microphone, listen through the speakers, and view the video window.

8. Inform your customer that you are going to share your customer service database.

9. Choose Tools → Share Application from the menu bar, or click the Share button in the main toolbar. (Make sure that the application is running first.)

10. Click the database, and a dialog box appears.

11. Click OK.

12. Click the database in the Windows status bar.

13. Click Collaborate in the main toolbar.

14. Arrange your desktop space so that you can access other NetMeeting features and controls, as shown in Figure 10-4.

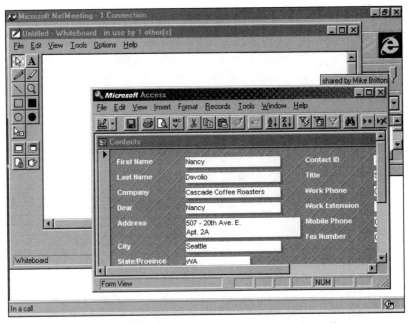

Figure 10-4 Arranging your desktop for a customer service call.

15. Double-click in the Shared Application window to take control of the cursor.

16. Enter the appropriate information or have the customer enter the information.

17. When you have completed keying the customer service information, choose **Tools** → **Share Application** from the menu bar.

18. Tell the user to click the database to stop sharing.

19. Continue the customer service call, accessing other features of NetMeeting or the database as needed.

20. When you have concluded the call, click Hang Up from the main toolbar.

21. You are now ready to make another call or exit the program. To make another call, just follow the previous instructions. To exit the program, choose **Call** → **Exit** from the menu bar.

Conducting Virtual Technical Support

In most cases, you will receive a technical support call from a frantic user that can't perform his or her job because of a computer problem. When you use NetMeeting, you can solve many of the software problems without physically going to the user. This will save valuable time and effort.

TIP If the help desk call arrives over the phone rather than through NetMeeting, you can assume that the problem is so severe that a personal visit to the user is needed. Keep this in mind when setting up your process. If the call comes through NetMeeting, it is probably software-related and can be solved in a virtual technical support call.

Follow these steps to make a virtual help desk call:

1. An incoming dialog box will appear on your computer. The dialog box gives you the option of accepting the call or ignoring the call. To answer the call, click Accept.

2. When you accept the call, the Connection window will list you and the troubled user. If you have video capabilities, you will see yourself and a frantic person trying to perform his or her job responsibilities on a computer that doesn't work.

3. If you have trouble hearing or if your voice is distorted, you can use the Audio toolbar to adjust the microphone and the speaker volume. Move the sliders to the right to increase the volume; move them to the left to decrease the volume. You can also adjust the camera if the image is not adequate.

4. After you have made all the necessary adjustments, you are ready to help solve the problem. Talk into the microphone, listen through the speakers, and view the video window.

5. Try to assess the severity of the problem.

6. Inform the user that you need to take control of their computer.

7. Ask the user to launch Windows Explorer from the Start menu, as shown in Figure 10-5.

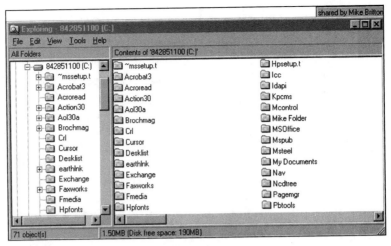

Figure 10-5 Launching Windows Explorer.

8. Tell the user to choose **Tools** → **Share Application** from the menu bar in NetMeeting, or tell them to click the Share button in the main toolbar.

9. Ask the user to click Windows Explorer, and a dialog box will appear.

10. Tell the user to click OK.

11. Ask the user to click Windows Explorer in the Windows status bar.

12. Tell the user to click Collaborate in the main toolbar.

13. Ask the user to maximize the Windows Explorer window, and then tell the user to sit back and relax while you solve the problem.

14. Arrange your desktop space so that you can access other NetMeeting features and controls.

15. Double-click in the Windows Explorer shared window to take control of the cursor. You now have complete control of the user's computer.

16. Diagnose and fix the problem as if you were at the remote computer. Ask the user to help if the process requires any physical steps, such as loading a diskette.

17. When you have completed the task, ask the user to choose **Tools** → **Share Application** from the menu bar.

18. Click Windows Explorer to stop sharing.

19. Make sure the problem is solved, and then log the information into the help desk database.

20. When you have concluded the call, click Hang Up from the main toolbar.

21. You are now ready to answer another call or exit the program.

BONUS

Using the Whiteboard to Create a Virtual Catalog

Have you ever examined the printing cost of your catalog? If you have, you already know that it's quite an expense. Even worse is the fact that as soon as your catalog is printed, it's out of date. To compound the costs, your catalog has to be shipped to your customer. And what about those new items that you want to sell? They need to wait until the next catalog.

Using NetMeeting's Whiteboard feature can help you solve this dilemma. When you use the File Transfer feature, you can always have an updated catalog ready to be displayed in a virtual customer service call, or ready to be sent electronically to your customer.

To create a virtual catalog by using the Whiteboard, follow these steps:

1. From the Current Call tab, click the Whiteboard icon on the main toolbar.

2. Copy and paste a scan of each item in your catalog onto a separate Whiteboard page, as shown in Figure 10-6.

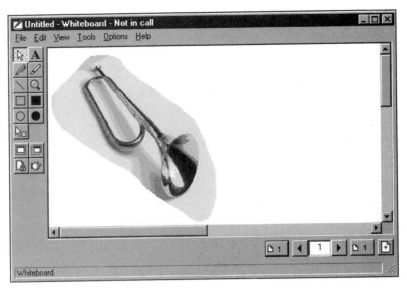

Figure 10-6 Creating a virtual catalog.

3. Click the Text Tool and enter the appropriate sales information concerning the item on each page, as shown in Figure 10-7.

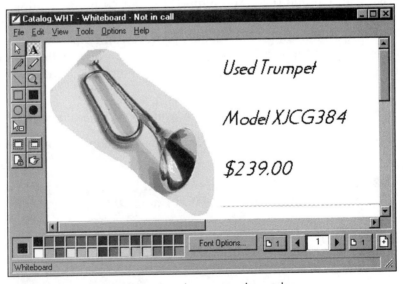

Figure 10-7 Adding the appropriate text to the catalog.

4. Save the Whiteboard and name it **Catalog**.

5. Add, delete, and update information as necessary.

6. Launch NetMeeting and connect to a ULS server, as described in Chapter 1.

7. Address and connect to a customer.

8. Inform the customer that you are going to launch the Whiteboard.

9. Press Control+W.

10. Arrange your workspace.

11. Choose **File** → **Open** from the Whiteboard menu.

12. Click Catalog to open your catalog.

13. Guide the customer to the appropriate pages and answer questions.

14. Click the Remote Pointer icon and the Highlight tool to emphasize your message, as shown in Figure 10-8.

Figure 10-8 Using the Remote Pointer to emphasize a product.

15. Use the other NetMeeting features as needed to provide customer service.

16. Choose **File** → **Exit** to leave the Whiteboard feature.

Summary

I n this chapter, you learned how to plan for virtual customer service and technical support. You learned the steps to implement a sound customer service and technical support solution, and you discovered the steps in conducting a customer service and technical support call.

In the next chapter, you'll learn how you can do your job from home. Whether it be customer service, technical support, or acccounting, telecommuting will help lower your costs and increase the flexibility of your company.

CHAPTER ELEVEN

TELECOMMUTING

IN THIS CHAPTER YOU LEARN THESE KEY SKILLS

UNDERSTANDING THE PROS AND CONS OF
TELECOMMUTING   PAGE 189

PLANNING FOR TELECOMMUTING   PAGE 191

BUYING THE RIGHT HARDWARE   PAGE 192

CONNECTING TO AN INTERNET SERVICE PROVIDER
PAGE 193

Telecommuting is a growing option for many companies, especially larger ones located in congested urban areas where commuting times continue to increase. With a combination of technology tools including voice lines, modem lines, video cameras, and messaging systems, you can work at home and keep in close contact with the corporate office.

NOTE   **For a preview of a few of the important features you'll find in this chapter, turn to the Discovery Center. You can use the page references in the Discovery Center to quickly find additional information.**

Telecommuting: The Pros and Cons

Telecommuting can be a terrific alternative to sitting on the freeway for hours a day — consider how refreshing it can be to roll out of bed, boot up your computer, and immediately be in business. Your company may support telecommuting one day a week or more; or you may consider transitioning from employee to contractor and work at home all the time.

You have more flexibility in your schedule, doing your work when it's best for you — whether you function better in the early morning, need a midday workout break, or need to drive the kids somewhere in the afternoon. By telecommuting, you can be freed from the chains of a 9 to 5 routine.

By not having to commute, you can lower costs because you're not traveling, eating pricey lunches, or needing an extensive wardrobe. You can lower your stress level because you're not rushing around to get out of the house; you can avoid sitting in traffic jams to get over the bridge, through the tunnel or toll, and other obstacles; and you don't have to face the lunch-time battle to run your errands along with everyone else.

> **TIP** Some people behave according to their attire. For example, hanging out in sneakers and sweats may not bring out your most professional attitude on the phone. Some telecommuters go through their same morning routine, even as far as a dress shirt and tie, before settling in front of their computer. It's up to you — but beware of the dawn of video conferencing.

You can be more productive working at home if you've got the discipline to stay focused. But, if you're the kind of person who gets distracted by laundry that's piled up, dishes that need to be washed, a soap opera that begs to be watched, or your beloved dog who wants your attention, working at home is going to be a challenge. You're going to have to find a way to overcome temptations: Perhaps you should seclude yourself from everything and everyone during what you consider "work hours." Or you commit to finishing a specific task or working a set number of hours before tackling the laundry or taking Fido out for a walk.

The other downside of telecommuting affects workaholic-type personalities. The office is always there, in your home, at 6 A.M., 10 P.M., and on weekends — those times when you probably should be focusing on your family instead of a sales report. You've got to know when to "close" the office, whether you consider yourself caught up on your work or not.

Telecommuting requires you to be more organized and self-motivated than the ordinary office worker who's regularly reminded of due dates and impending projects. You've got to be able to prioritize on your own, and know when to call for additional resources and/or support. And you've got to be able to report on your progress regularly, whether it's a formal status report or a casual update, to ensure that your colleagues know you're working at home instead of chasing the cat and watching *All My Children*.

Planning for Telecommuting

Setting up your home office is a critical first step to being a successful telecommuter. You'll need to designate a quick area of your home or apartment, preferably one with a door that you can close at the end of your work day.

TIP Remember that a home office can be a tax deduction. It's important that it be a distinctly separate room dedicated to the business and not used by you or your family for personal matters. You may be able to deduct a percentage that's the proportion of office space to living space, usually 25 to 33 percent. Consult your tax professional for details.

An example of a productive and comfortable home office is shown in Figure 11-1. You'll need to obtain the following items:

* **A desk:** Pick one that's the right height for you to work on a computer, and one that still gives you space for paper. We aren't fully digital yet.

* **A comfortable ergonomic chair.** Forget those "executive" high back chairs — get a working person's chair with a contoured back and cushioned arms if you do a lot of computer work.

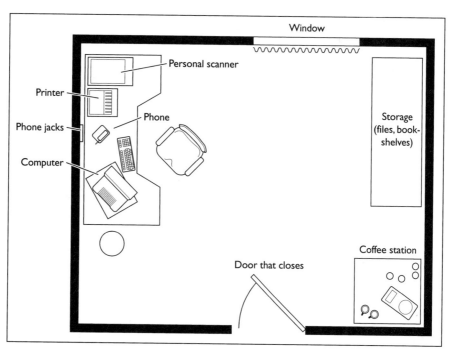

Figure 11-1 A sample floorplan for a well-designed home office.

* **Phone lines:** You'll need to be separate from your family phone line, and get two additional phone lines if you can: one for voice and one for a computer. If it's available in your area, consider getting an ISDN line or even a T-1 line for faster speed and bandwidth. You can have both voice and modem on one ISDN line, so compare the costs before you write off ISDN.

Check out the availability of phone lines before renting an apartment or buying a house. Some rental complexes prohibit any additional external wiring, which means you may be limited to one or two phone lines. If you're buying an older home, you may have trouble getting more than two lines, depending on the area. Check with the local phone company for details — rental agents and brokers often won't understand the importance of the issue and may casually dismiss the question.

* **Environment:** Remember that you'll spend a lot of time in this room when you're telecommuting. Make your environment professional and pleasant. Get as much light as you can, add familiar things like photos, plants, or other items that make you feel comfortable.
* **Coffee break items:** Some people tend to get really distracted if they saunter off to the kitchen to make a cup of coffee. You may want to get a coffee maker and small refrigerator for your office to avoid that temptation.

Buying the Right Hardware

Of course, your computer is the centerpiece of your home office. You'll need a computer with the following:

* **Adequate RAM:** A minimum of 16 megs, 32 preferred. You'll want to be multitasking — that is, working in Microsoft Word (a RAM hog!), online to the Internet with NetMeeting, calculating projections in a spreadsheet, and so on — all at the same time.
* **A big hard drive:** Between Internet downloads, software, and files to and from the office, you'll need a lot of storage space. Get a 1 gigabyte drive, minimum.
* **Sound and video:** Make sure you get a sound card (some PCs sold as office computers don't include these, and adding them afterward is a hassle), and consider buying a video camera (but remember then that working in your feetie pajamas is out!).

* **A big monitor:** Get a 17-inch monitor even though it costs more. Your eyes will thank you for it, and you'll see a lot more in your conferences.

* **A modem:** Get one that's as fast as is available; the latest standard for regular phone lines is 33.6 baud. ISDN lines require a digital modem.

* **A personal scanner:** Consider buying a PaperPort or another small desktop scanner for digitizing those odd pieces of paper that need to get to someone else in a hurry. It's also a lot easier to file digital information than paper. These scanners cost about $299.

* **A printer:** If you do a lot of printing, or print large graphic files of charts or pictures, spring for a laser printer. An ink jet printer is fine for casual use, but it will take several minutes per page for graphics.

Hooking Up with an Internet Service Provider

Finally, you'll need to set up access to the Internet by choosing an Internet Service Provider (ISP). ISPs vary by the following:

* **Access numbers:** That is, the local phone number you dial for access, and how often you'll get a busy signal at that number. This is probably the most critical criteria for the telecommuter — if you can't connect, you're not in business.

* **Monthly usage rates:** Some ISPs offer fixed rates for unlimited use averaging $19.95 per month. Others offer a flat fee, about $9.95 for the first five hours, and then about $2.95 per hour thereafter.

* **Amount of storage included:** This is useful if you're creating your own Web pages. Some ISPs include enough storage for a Web page or two, others include a megabyte.

Shop around before picking an ISP. You've probably heard complaints about many of the providers, and a lot of that is due to tremendous and unanticipated growth. Some ISPs and their contact information can be found in Table 11-1.

TABLE 11-1   Contacting ISPs

ISP	Web address	Phone
AT&T WORLDNET	http://www.att.com/worldnet	800-967-5363
EARTHLINK	http://www.earthlink.net	800-395-8425

(continued)

TABLE 11-1 Contacting ISPs

ISP	Web address	Phone
GTE INTERNET SOLUTIONS	http://www.gte.net	800-363-8483
IBM INTERNET CONNECTION	http://www.ibm.net	800-455-5056
MCI INTERNET	http://www.mci2000.com	800-550-0927
NETCOM	http://www.netcom.com	800-353-6600
SPRYNET	http://www.sprynet.com	800-777-9638

BONUS

Tips for Successful Telecommuting

To be a successful telecommuter, consider these tips:

1. Set ground rules with your family to minimize interruptions during work hours. Set up a system for them to leave you messages that you can address during a break.

2. Never leave your phone unanswered. Get a voice messaging service so your voice mail picks up even if you're on the phone. Make sure you can access your voice mail remotely, and get a call forwarding feature. Consider buying a cellular phone if you're on the move a lot.

3. Set up your e-mail to automatically pick up your mail hourly. Respond as soon as possible.

4. Keep track of your time. You'll be surprised to see how you're spending your day, and you'll get ideas of how to be more productive.

5. Practice good file management, especially when you're moving files between a corporate office computer and your home computer. If you're using Windows 95, consider using the Briefcase feature to manage your files. Or, think about getting a notebook with a docking station so that you're always using the same computer.

6. Back up your files regularly. Remember that you don't have someone in Systems backing up the data from your home computer.

7. Prioritize your work so that you're doing individual projects at home, and those that require participation from others while you're at the office.

8. Make the transition slowly, starting with one day a week and increasing it as it seems workable. Treat telecommuting as a privilege and don't abuse it by taking the day off to golf.

Summary

In this chapter, you learned the pros and cons of telecommuting, depending on your nature and work habits. You also learned how to plan for telecommuting, including setting up your home office, buying the right hardware, including computer and peripheral devices. You discovered how to find and connect to an Internet Service Provider.

In the next chapter, you'll discover how to learn from the Internet while at home.

12

Imagine learning without the hassles: no commuting to a central institution, more control over the hours you spend in a classroom, easily accessible resources online. Consider the advantages of being able to communicate to fellow students, anytime, virtually anywhere in the world. The idea of distance learning is just at the beginning stages, and promises to change the way we learn, whether it's an academic, corporate, or recreational subject.

NOTE For a preview of a few of the **important features you'll find in this chapter, turn to the Discovery Center. You can use the page references in the Discovery Center to quickly find additional information.**

Anytime, Anywhere Learning

Distance learning is the idea that you can learn within your own space and time via online access. That means you don't have to travel to your local community college every Wednesday evening and cram the week's worth of information into a four-hour period after a long day of work. Distance learning means that you won't have to travel to your corporate headquarters for new product or skill training. And it means you can fine-tune your basket weaving skills without ever leaving your home.

Distance learning combines the following technologies for effective education:

* **Discussion groups:** Participants can share information by posting questions, answers, and queries about the subject in a common "database" that's accessible online. Participants can post a question to the group, answer someone else's question, or simply read the comments of others.

* **Chat groups:** These are interactive, with all participants being online at the same time and having a dialog of words on the screen. The chat group can be moderated by an instructor or tutor to focus and enhance the chat.

* **Video and audio conferencing:** With these tools, you can see and hear multiple participants in the session, just like being in the same classroom.

* **Whiteboard:** "Show" ideas with the Whiteboard feature, whether you show freeform sketches or detailed diagrams. Plus, all participants can instantly have a copy for future reference.

* **E-mail:** Participants can one-on-one e-mail other students, exchanging notes, ideas, and so on.

* **Online resources:** Participants can have virtually instantaneous access to a wealth of online information, including a log of homework assignments, reference works, and resources.

Planning for Distance Learning

Taking an online course is pretty easy — you'll just have to register with some general contact information, and plunk down your credit card if you have to pay for the course. You'll also have to get the necessary materials; some are available electronically and some can be ordered online.

If you're the one providing the online "course," you've got a lot more to do. The course can be a simple informative session about a new product, a comprehensive sales training program, or an ongoing forum for continuing education. To conduct an online course, you'll need to do the following:

* **Establish the subject.** Clearly define the goals and scope of the course. Create an outline and distribute it so that everyone knows what to expect, in terms of what they'll learn and what they'll need to do.

* **Establish the audience.** Define who the course is appropriate for. For example, you don't want a corporate vice-president signing up for an

introductory office management course. At the same time, you don't want your new hires poking around in budget analysis before their time.

* **Establish the communication method.** Decide which of the online tools will work best for your subject matter: chat groups, discussion groups, e-mail, or other online forums. Your decision will depend on the geographical location and time constraints of participants as well as the importance of the course to your organization. For example, if the course is on how to prepare next year's budgets, and participation is mandatory, you will have a lot more authority to make demands from your participants.

* **Establish the time frame.** Clarify how much time participants will have to spend, both online and offline, to achieve the goals of the course.

* **Prepare the course.** Create an outline and create modules for your course. By creating it in pieces, participants can digest the material instead of being overwhelmed by a mountain of information. Distribute the material in a readable format, whether it's in Web pages on your intranet — Adobe Acrobat .PDF files that can be read, searched, and annotated — or a textual file in a format that everyone can read.

TIP Remember that Web pages and Acrobat pages retain the structure and formatting of your document. Web browsers and the Acrobat Reader application are easily available to anyone with Web access.

* **Promote the session.** Let people know about your online course. You may try promoting a short, simple course to get them to try out the new mode of learning.

Conducting an Online Course

After you've done all the planning, you're ready to conduct your online course. Treat the course like any other educational and training forum by following these tips:

* **Be on time and be a role model.** As the course leader, you set the tone for the class, in terms of your timeliness, responsiveness, and behavior online.

* **Keep it interesting.** Add stories and case studies as much as possible so participants can see examples of the theory applied in the real world.

* **Invite interaction as much as possible.** Emphasize participation in chat groups and discussion groups, with or without moderation from you or a mentor.

* **Solicit feedback.** Ask your students what worked well, and what didn't. Find out if they achieve their goals. Ask what topics they'd like to see covered in the future and find out if they would recommend the course to their colleagues.

 For details on connecting participants for chat groups, see Chapter 6. For details on connecting participants for a video conference, see Chapter 7. For details on using the Whiteboard feature, see Chapter 5.

BONUS

Experience Distance Learning

Just what is it like to learn online? To answer that question, try it yourself on the World Wide Web at DigitalThink's Web site, which includes a free demonstration course just for registering.

The site builds on the school metaphor, as shown in Figure 12-1, with a locker that contains a chat lobby, a discussion lobby, your student profile, the courses in which you're enrolled, and more. DigitalThink uses ichat, shown in Figure 12-2, for live interactive chat rooms. Course participants can exchange ideas and information in this forum, which is periodically moderated by the course instructor.

 Visit DigitalThink at http://www.digitalthink.com.

DigitalThink's discussion groups enable participants to post questions, answers, comments, and other information. These discussion groups are organized by topics around the courses, promoting interaction between participants regardless of geographic location or time of day.

DigitalThink's learning environment includes access to a tutor, quizzes, and scores of classmates so you can chart your progress relative to other students in the course. You can access additional resources, just like going to the school library, only much faster and more comprehensively. Finally, some DigitalThink courses include corresponding course materials, such as books, software, and Web links. Give it a try!

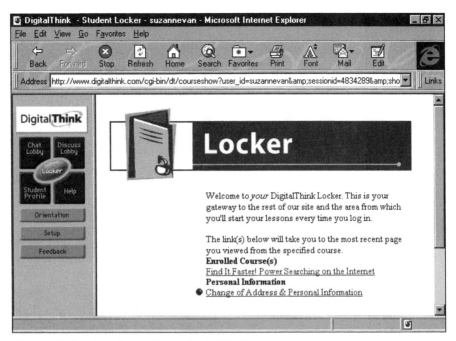

Figure 12-1 A student locker at DigitalThink.

Figure 12-2 DigitalThink's ichat for online chatting.

Summary

In this chapter, you learned how chat groups, discussion groups, whiteboards, video and audio conferencing, and e-mail technologies are being utilized for distance learning. You also learned how to plan a distance learning course for your organization's educational needs and how to conduct an online learning course.

In the next chapter, you'll discover how to find love on the Net as you learn how to use NetMeeting's capabilities to enhance your personal life.

BENEFITS OF NETMEETING

What can NetMeeting do for you? What benefits can you derive from desktop conferencing software? Part Three details the obvious — and not so obvious — benefits of using NetMeeting and desktop conferencing from both a personal and a professional perspective. You also get invaluable advice on making the most of your NetMeeting experiences.

For Renee and Howard, NetMeeting has been a saving grace to their relationship, their financial future, and their sanity. Both of them had worked together for the same US-based corporation for many years. However, they didn't quite realize the attraction they had for each other until Howard accepted a three-year assignment in London just around the same time that Renee was promoted and agreed to relocate to the company's New York headquarters.

With Howard in London and Renee in New York, their relationship continued to blossom throughout the fall — but so did their phone bills. Although at one point their bills were up to $500 per month, they still felt that they couldn't spend enough time talking to each other. Long weekends enabled them to take turns flying across the Atlantic to see one another, but the airfare and time-zone changes started taking their toll before too long.

By February, Renee was at wit's end and ready to quit her job, even though she knew she wouldn't be able to find comparable work in London. Until a Valentine's Day gift from Howard arrived: a desktop video camera and directions for downloading Microsoft NetMeeting. "I was appalled, at first" Renee says, "but that's probably because I was expecting something small and shiny — about a carat's worth!"

After cooling down for a bit and being encouraged by a Net-surfing girlfriend, Renee fired up the camera and logged onto the Internet. She found Howard online, and they began chatting away in a new dimension with visual cues as well as words. They were able to see each other right on their monitors, send pictures of their apartments and their families back and forth, and use the Whiteboard to draw sweet nothings to each other. Before too long, they were hooked.

Even though they talked every night their phone bills dropped incredibly because all they now had to pay was a monthly usage fee to their online service providers.

By May, they were so impressed with their find that they took the concept to their employer, and subsequently championed a corporate program for desktop video conferencing. Of course, the program required Renee to visit London to sell the idea, and visit her beau at the same time.

CHAPTER THIRTEEN

USING NETMEETING IN YOUR PERSONAL LIFE

IN THIS CHAPTER YOU LEARN THESE KEY SKILLS

13

There are many benefits for businesses that use NetMeeting, as you will see in the next chapter. However, you can have a lot of fun using NetMeeting in your personal life as well. Imagine talking with a new friend in Japan, sending your recent photos to relatives, or video conferencing with a college student that's miles away from home. All of these can easily be accomplished with NetMeeting.

This chapter gives you some ideas for making NetMeeting your personal communication tool. You also discover some practical steps, tips, and tricks to customize NetMeeting, resulting in lower costs. So sit back and discover the personal world of NetMeeting.

NOTE For a preview of a few of the important features you'll find in this chapter, turn to the Discovery Center. You can use the page references in the Discovery Center to quickly find additional information.

Keeping in Touch with Friends and Family

How's your long-distance phone bill? No doubt pretty big if you have a friend or family member that lives in another area code. You could easily be spending hundreds of dollars each month phoning one friend once or twice a week! What if you could talk, see, and write to that friend anytime you want, for as long as you want, and only pay the cost of your Internet Service Provider? Well, that's what NetMeeting allows you to do. Although telephone companies will probably try to stop this activity in the future, today you can reduce that hundred-dollar phone bill to twenty dollars and have unlimited fun and communication with the ones you love. All you have to do is "reach out and click somebody." The next section shows you exactly how to do it.

Finding Your Friends on NetMeeting

When you use the User Location Service directory you can find friends that are connected and ready to talk with you on NetMeeting. Unfortunately, you cannot search for a particular name within NetMeeting; it would make finding your friends a very easy process. However, you can do a couple of work-arounds to assist you. First, you can sort the ULS directory so that you have an alphabetical list through which you can scroll. Second, you can place your friends in your SpeedDial directory, and NetMeeting will automatically tell you if they are logged on.

 X-REF See Chapter 8 if you forgot what the ULS does.

To find a friend by sorting by Last Name, follow these steps:

1. Click the Directory tab in the main NetMeeting window, as shown in Figure 13-1.

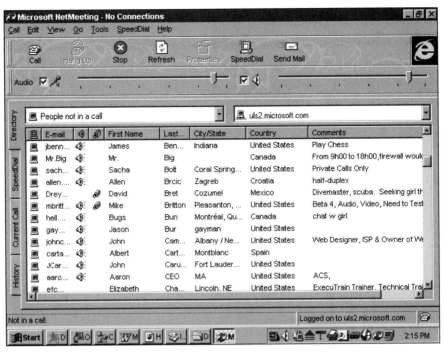

Figure 13-1 The Directory tab.

2. Click the ULS server to which you want to connect. NetMeeting automatically connects you to that directory server.

   The dynamic ULS directory appears in the Directory window. If you chose your ULS, you will find your name among those in the directory, as shown in Figure 13-2.

3. Click the Last Name field in the ULS directory window. NetMeeting sorts the field in alphabetical order from A to Z.

4. Click the field name again. NetMeeting sorts the field from Z to A.

5. Scroll through the list to find a friend to call.

6. Follow the instructions in Chapter 2 to place the call.

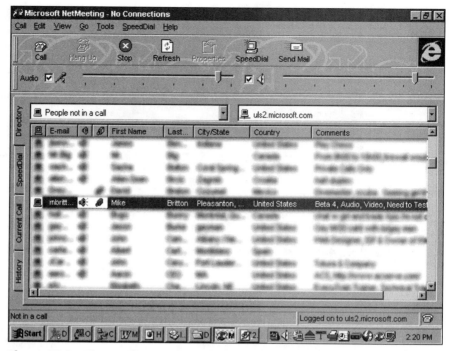

Figure 13-2 The ULS directory showing your name among those not in a conference.

To find a friend by using SpeedDial, follow these steps:

1. Click the SpeedDial tab in the main NetMeeting window. The friends who you have placed in this directory appear, as shown in Figure 13-3.

2. Look in the Status column to find out whether or not your friend is logged on.

3. In the Name column, click the name of the friend you want to call.

4. Click **Call** on the menu bar. NetMeeting places an Internet phone call to your friend.

TIP There are many ULS servers from which to choose, with many more being added daily. It takes several minutes for each ULS directory to be downloaded. If you have several friends located on several different servers, finding them can be a problem. A little coordination can be a great time-savings. If you and the friends you call most are listed in the same ULS directory, you only need to download the list once. Call your friends beforehand and make sure that everybody uses the same ULS. You can also call a friend by inputting his or her e-mail address in the call window; however, if your friend isn't logged onto his or her ISP, the call won't go through.

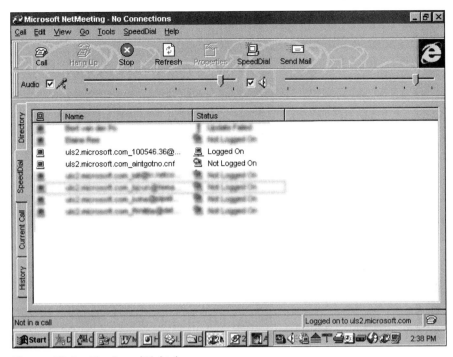

Figure 13-3 The SpeedDial tab.

A NetMeeting Family Reunion

The family reunion is an American institution. It usually happens every 5 to 10 years. In some families, a reunion is an annual event. If you have ever been involved in planning and coordinating one of these gatherings, you know just how much time, effort, money, and frustration is involved in making the event a success. If you have ever attended a reunion, you understand the travel expense, the logistics, and the tension that can be placed on a family. NetMeeting isn't a replacement for personal interaction between family members, yet it can be used to facilitate the planning of a reunion. In some cases, it could be the mechanism for holding the reunion or linking in those who physically can't make it.

TIP When sending out the invitations for your next family reunion, include instructions for downloading and using NetMeeting. Offer this as an alternative to physically attending the reunion. You might even suggest buying this book for complete details.

College Students Phone Home

You probably have seen the television commercials selling personal 800 numbers for college students. Phone companies know that this is a huge market. Students leave home, get homesick, run up large phone bills, and of course don't have any extra money so Mom and Dad end up paying the bill. The 800 number makes it easier for the student to phone home.

NetMeeting can help you eliminate this monthly charge and allow you to talk and visit using video. Most college students own a computer and have an Internet Service Provider. Adding the needed hardware, approximately $300, enables you to see and speak with them for no additional long-distance charge.

 The video feature of NetMeeting requires some getting used to. Imagine viewing that college dorm room on a day-to-day basis. It's probably not a pretty site. A conventional phone call hides the mess; a video call is like a picture window into the room. Remember, if you have the video featured configured along with the Auto Answer feature, you can look at the dorm room anytime you want. On second thought, it may be safer to disable the Auto Answer feature!

Reducing Phone Bills and Travel Expenses

A video conference is the next best thing to being there, but it doesn't replace personal interaction. However, the cost of being there goes up proportionately with the distance from home. Imagine living in New York and having a loved one in Australia. The minimum cost of a personal visit would be several thousand dollars. Even a phone call can be quite expensive. A little forward planning, an Internet connection, and some hardware can really make a financial difference and keep a distance-separated family together.

Finding and Making New Acquaintances

Communicating with friends and family with NetMeeting is a fantastic way to stay in touch. But the world doesn't totally revolve around the ones you currently know. There are many new voices and faces to discover. With NetMeeting, you can circle the globe in a matter of seconds, find exotic new friends, and even talk with the guy just down the block.

A World of New Acquaintances

How do you make new friends? What sociological circumstance happens that makes two people want to share with one another? Friendship is a complicated issue. However, one thing is for sure: There's usually a common denominator between friends. Friends have a common interest, a mutual goal, or a collective belief. Finding that common denominator can be quite difficult. You need to be in the right place at the right time to make it happen.

NetMeeting can facilitate friendship. Everyone connected to a ULS already has a common interest — you know, that technological bond that brings people together. Even if they don't speak your language, the drawing capabilities of the Whiteboard allow you to communicate.

International Pen Pals

Did you ever have a pen pal, writing a letter every week or even every day? With NetMeeting, you can travel the globe in search of a new friend, without ever leaving your computer keyboard. The "Bonus" section of Chapter 8 gives you complete instructions for making an international connection. For your convenience though, here is an abbreviated set of steps.

Follow these steps to find an international pen pal:

1. Click the Directory tab.

2. Click the ULS server to whom you want to connect.

3. Position the cursor on the Country field in the ULS directory window.

4. Click the Country field name.

5. Scroll down the list to view the users from different countries, as shown in Figure 13-4.

6. Double-click the name of your potential international pen pal.

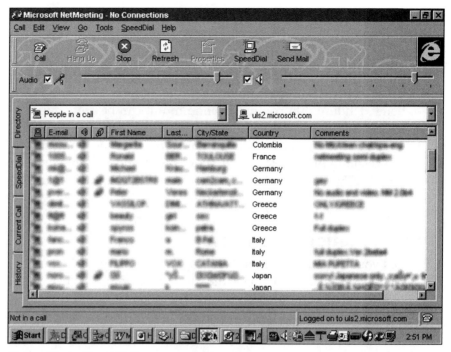

Figure 13-4 The ULS directory sorted by country.

Searching for That Special Love

With NetMeeting, not only can you find a foreign pen pal, you can find your one true love. That's right, a click on a name in the ULS directory can be the first step toward a lasting relationship. Well, maybe NetMeeting won't replace a real date, but it's fun to try.

Love at First Click

You've heard of love at first sight. Well, using NetMeeting is love at first click. Connecting to a potential love candidate is simple. Follow the instructions in Chapter 2 for making an Internet phone call. If you have video capabilities, you can see the future person of your dreams. But how do you differentiate those "lookin' for love" from those who want to share their spreadsheet application? The answer lies in the Comment section of the ULS directory window. Figure 13-5 shows some typical comments.

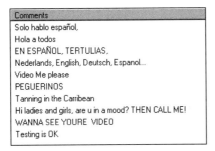

Figure 13-5 The Comments window of the ULS directory.

```
Comments
Solo hablo español,
Hola a todos
EN ESPAÑOL, TERTULIAS,
Nederlands, English, Deutsch, Espanol...
Video Me please
PEGUERINOS
Tanning in the Carribean
Hi ladies and girls, are u in a mood? THEN CALL ME!
WANNA SEE YOURE VIDEO
Testing is OK
```

By scrolling through the Comment section, you can easily assess those who have love on the brain.

At the writing of this book, the Comment section in the ULS directory is not censored. In many cases, the messages written there are X-rated and there is no way of blocking them. Use your best judgment when contacting someone who displays a vulgar message. If the person is bold enough to write filth in the Comment section, you can be assured that any communication will be of that nature as well.

Advertising Your Intentions

NetMeeting allows you to customize your personal information to suit your current needs. This information is displayed in the Comment section of the ULS directory. By carefully crafting a witty comment, you can attract the appropriate response.

To customize your personal information, follow these steps:

1. Choose Tools → Options from the menu bar. The NetMeeting Options window appears.

2. Click the My Info tab to access your personal preferences, as shown in Figure 13-6.

3. Enter your first name in the First name box.

4. Enter your last name in the Last name box.

5. Enter your e-mail address in the E-mail address box. This entry can only contain letters, numbers, and some symbols. E-mail names cannot contain characters such as "< > /".

6. Enter your city and state in the City/State box.

7. Click in the pop-up window and select the country in which you reside.

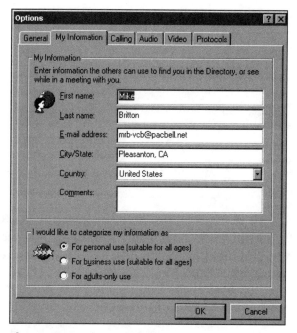

Figure 13-6   The My Information tab.

8. Enter any personal comments that you want others to read, as shown in Figure 13-7.

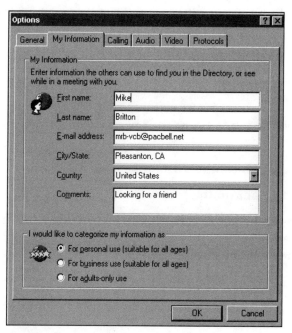

Figure 13-7   Enter personal comments in the Comments field.

9. Click OK. Your comment now appears in the Directory tab when you refresh the display, as shown in Figure 13-8.

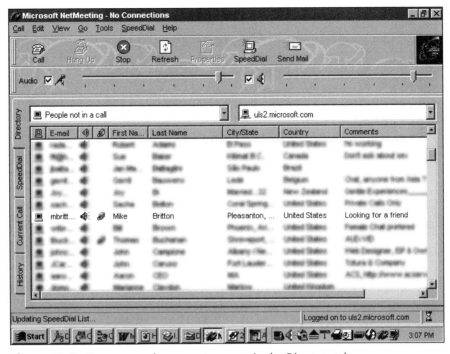

Figure 13-8 Your personal comments appear in the Directory tab.

IRL Versus URL

Nothing beats IRL relationships (you know, In Real Life). However, NetMeeting can be the beginning of a URL relationship if done with the proper precautions.

Follow these guidelines when considering a NetMeeting love life:

1. Be cautious when entering personal information; there are wicked people out there that want to take advantage of you.

2. Carefully consider not contacting someone that displays an X-rated message in the Comment section. The Comment field gives you a glimpse of the person's personality.

3. Never give out your home address or any other personal information over the Internet.

4. Never configure NetMeeting to automatically answer with the video feature. You may not be ready to be in pictures.

5. When you do find that special someone on NetMeeting, list both on the same ULS server. It will simplify the connection process.

Using NetMeeting for Entertainment

Y ou don't have to have a mission to use NetMeeting. It's not necessary for you to have a friend, be a friend, or need a friend. You can just sit back, relax, and wait on some of the most interesting people on the planet to contact you. Or you can actively surf through the vast array of current NetMeeting users and find some very odd things.

Surfing the Phone Book

Surfing the phone book is a lot of fun. Simply connect to NetMeeting, as described in earlier chapters, and sort by Comment. Scroll through the wacky listings until you find one that is of interest. You never know what you'll find (see Figure 13-9).

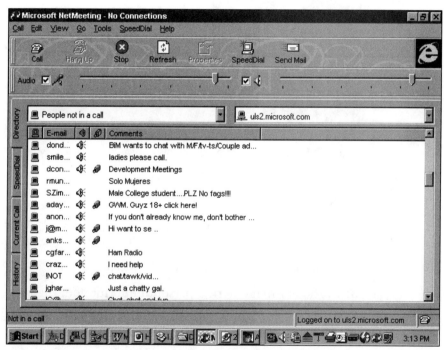

Figure 13-9 Almost anything is written in the Comment section.

Current Weather in Africa

By changing your Comment field, you can be entertained for hours. For instance, why not type **Is it raining where you are?** Doing this will result in many exotic replies, even from as far away as Africa. You may not be able to understand the verbal language, but if you are using the Whiteboard, you can still communicate. See Figure 13-10; it shows an actual Whiteboard drawing from a NetMeeting user in Africa.

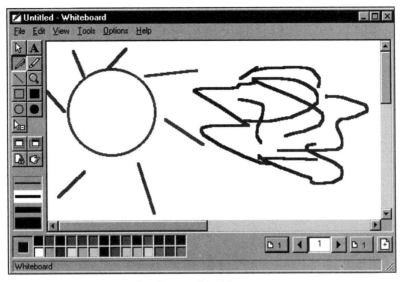

Figure 13-10 The weather forecast in Africa.

Use your imagination to solicit any type of response that you want, but remember: Whatever you solicit, you'll get on NetMeeting.

Research with NetMeeting

Besides surfing the ULS for entertainment, you can zoom around the planet in search of information. If you are writing a paper for school, researching facts for a business presentation, or even writing a book on NetMeeting, the virtual conference features will come in very handy.

Instant Information

The ULS directory contains some very knowledgeable people on almost any subject. You probably have used a search engine on the Internet to obtain static information placed on Web pages. NetMeeting puts life into this information by allowing you to communicate with the person who created it. Imagine being able to ask a question to a rocket scientist or listen to a philosopher first-hand. Virtual conferencing will enhance almost any search for data.

The Next Picasso

When you use the Whiteboard feature, you can see graphical information. For example, you can see scans of existing artwork or even an on-the-fly piece created by a budding artist just for you. Just follow the steps explained in previous chapters to save this artwork, print it, or paste it into other applications. With these graphics, you can even create your very own greeting.

BONUS

Creating and Sending a NetMeeting Postcard

You can create your very own greeting to be used when looking for new friends, or you can keep in touch with existing friends and family. When you use the Whiteboard feature, you can display your creativity online, or even send the Whiteboard file by using e-mail.

To create a NetMeeting postcard, follow these steps:

1. Choose Tools → Whiteboard , or press Control+W.

2. Copy and paste a scan onto the Whiteboard, as shown in Figure 13-11.

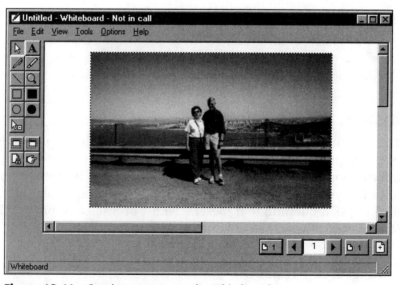

Figure 13-11   Copying a scan onto the Whiteboard.

3. Click the Text Tool and type **Greetings from San Francisco**, or whatever you want your message to be, as shown in Figure 13-12.

4. Choose File → Save from the menu bar and enter a file name.

Figure 13-12 Adding a greeting to your postcard.

Summary

In this chapter, you discovered some of the personal benefits that come with using NetMeeting. You can talk to friends and family. You can find new friends and lovers. You can entertain yourself, and you can do research. You can even lower your expenses.

In the next chapter, you learn how to put NetMeeting to work to benefit your professional life.

CHAPTER FOURTEEN

USING NETMEETING IN YOUR BUSINESS LIFE

IN THIS CHAPTER YOU LEARN THESE KEY SKILLS

A s you have just discovered, NetMeeting can be a lot of fun in your personal life. However, NetMeeting can also help your business life in many ways. In today's world, the demands on time and cost reduction are on every person's mind. Companies downsize to turn a profit, close divisions that don't perform to an expected level, and simply don't care about the lives of the employees they effect. The business world truly is a jungle.

NetMeeting can tame this jungle by lowering costs, reducing the physical demands on employees, and providing access to information on a real-time basis. In this chapter, you discover how to use NetMeeting to build a stronger business and become a happier employee.

NOTE   For a preview of a few of the important features you'll find in this chapter, turn to the Discovery Center. You can use the page references in the Discovery Center to quickly find additional information.

Reduce Travel Costs

Cost reduction seems to be the term of the 90's. Downsizing, layoffs, and restructuring are all results of reducing costs. One of the largest cost centers in a company is Travel and Entertainment. Whether you have a small home business or you are a part of a mega-company, you know the financial effects that business travel inflicts on your budget. The good news is that NetMeeting can help you lower these costs; you just have to understand how.

Analyze Your Current Travel Budget

The first step in lowering travel costs is to understand them. Take a good, long look at your travel costs. Use the five W's to help: Who, What, When, Where, and Why. Discover who travels and what business they conduct. Understand when they go and where they go. Finally, uncover the reason for the travel. Place all this information in a matrix, as shown in Figure 14-1. Suddenly patterns will emerge.

Staff Member	Travel Purpose	Destination	Date of Travel	Method of Travel
1				
2				
3				
4				
5				
6				
7				
8				
9				
10				

Figure 14-1   A travel matrix.

Analyze these patterns to determine if NetMeeting can lower your travel costs.

Reductions Using NetMeeting

Using the matrix in Figure 14-1, determine if the following scenarios exist in your company:

* One person travels to a remote location to visit one person.
* Groups of people travel to the same location for a meeting.
* The purpose of the travel is to share a presentation or information.
* The travel happens on a regular schedule.

If any of these scenarios exist in your company, NetMeeting can help reduce your travel costs.

ONE-ON-ONE MEETINGS

The expense of time and travel for one-on-one meetings can be very wasteful of resources. NetMeeting is designed to eliminate most of this cost. A one-on-one meeting can use all the features of NetMeeting: audio, video, data transfers, Whiteboard, and so forth. In most cases, there is no need to spend the money to travel. A properly configured NetMeeting conference will significantly reduce your travel budget.

THE BOARD MEETING

The only thing worse than sending a person across the country or world to a meeting is sending a group of people. This is called the Board Meeting effect. The total cost of the excursion doesn't just go up accordingly by the number of attendees. A group of people will always spend more money dining, socializing, and entertaining.

With the proper NetMeeting network, a typical Board Meeting can be conducted virtually. Although only the first two connections in NetMeeting have audio and video capabilities, you can use this to your advantage. By setting up the conference using Chat and the Whiteboard, you will usually reduce the amount of extraneous information. Not only will you reduce your travel costs, you'll reduce the length of the meeting and probably get more accomplished.

THE PRESENTATION

Many business trips are taken to share a presentation or some piece of information. NetMeeting is designed to do just that. When you use the Whiteboard, Application Sharing, and File Transfer features, you can conduct a great presentation without ever leaving your home or office. PowerPoint presentations are a natural with NetMeeting. Simply prepare the presentation as you would for display on your computer. Use the Application Sharing feature and the audio and video capabilities to give a fantastic presentation, all within the virtual meeting.

THE REGULAR MEETING

If you conduct regular meetings, NetMeeting can significantly lower your travel costs. Taking the time to install, configure, and test a NetMeeting network will pay off in the first meeting. However, you must be patient. The first time you use NetMeeting in a conference, there will be a learning curve. For many people, the thought of being on a video camera intimidates them. They develop a sense of "stage fright" that may cause your meeting to be disrupted. Some people will gravitate away from the camera and out of viewing range; others will simply not speak. Because virtual meetings are different than live meetings, you may want to practice. If the same group of people meet on a regular basis and use NetMeeting, the familiarity with the virtual conference will grow and the meetings will become more and more effective.

Side Effects

There is a side effect in using virtual meetings to reduce travel costs. People like to travel and they will look for ways to discredit anything that prevents them from spending the travel budget. Many people consider travel and entertainment to be part of their benefits. It is very easy to sabotage a NetMeeting conference. Keep this in mind when you use a virtual meeting to launch your cost-cutting measure, especially if your neck is on the line concerning the success of the virtual technology. Practice sessions, testing, and complete documentation of the process will ensure the success. Using NetMeeting can be a lot of fun. Play up the good aspects and try to minimize the negatives, such as the inevitable technical snafus.

Instant Access to People and Information

Having your assistant call another assistant to set up a lunch to discuss a matter is very inefficient; however, that's the way business is usually conducted. In addition, by the time the lunch arrives, your schedule has changed and your assistant must call the other assistant to reschedule the meeting. Whatever happened to personal, instant access to people and information? Voice mail talks to voice mail, and automatic e-mail responds to incoming messages. NetMeeting can help you get out of this vicious circle and get the information you need.

Analyze Your Current Communication Structure

What is the structure of your company's communication? Do you have voice mail and e-mail? Do you schedule every minute of your day in meetings? Take time to analyze how you communicate with others in your company and with your customers. Create a matrix, as shown in Figure 14-2. This will help you understand how you communicate so that you can determine how to use NetMeeting to get the information you need, when you need it.

When to Use NetMeeting

Review the findings from the communication matrix. If you find the following, NetMeeting can help you better access information:

* You have four or more meetings per day.
* You reply to the same e-mail more than once.
* You leave more than three voice-mail messages per day.

Staff Member	E-mail	Voice Mail	Personal Meetings
1			
2			
3			
4			

Staff Member	E-mail	Voice Mail	Personal Meetings
5			
6			
7			
8			
9			
10			

Figure 14-2 A communication matrix.

Better Customer Service

Your window to the world is customer service. Poor customer service can drive away existing customers and turn away new ones. Providing a higher level of customer support can do just the opposite. You will keep your valued customers and bring in new ones. However, you do need to understand the effectiveness of your current customer support.

Analyze Your Current Customer Service

Many companies don't understand why they lose customers, and even if they do, they can't afford to fix the problem. NetMeeting can provide a higher level of support without increasing costs. By using the features described in Chapter 10, any company can take advantage of virtual customer service, but you do need to understand your current situation.

When to Use NetMeeting

Take some time to analyze how your customer service works. Understand the dynamics of dealing with a wide variety of customers. Then use the following criteria to determine when to use NetMeeting to better service your customers. Consider using NetMeeting if

* The majority of your customers use e-mail.
* You sell and/or service a software product.
* A visual, personal communication is important.

By using the Audio, Video Conferencing, and Application Sharing features of NetMeeting, you can promote your customer service to new levels. It will take a little time, but the effort will be worth it.

Reduce Cost of Help Desk

Your internal technical support costs are either very high or you lack the support needed for your staff to function; there is no in-between. In today's technological world, anything and everything will go wrong and somebody has to fix it!

NetMeeting can provide the solution, the balance between the number of help desk employees needed, and the level of support required for maintenance.

Analyze Your Current Help Desk

Taking the time to analyze your current help desk performance will be an eye-opener. The simple survey shown in Figure 14-3 provides you with the information you need to determine if you need more staff or if NetMeeting can help solve your problem.

Help Desk Survey	Comment
Date of last Help Desk call	
Time from call to response	
Length of call	
Type of call (hardware/software)	
Resolution	

Figure 14-3 The help desk survey.

When to Use NetMeeting

Consider using NetMeeting to provide better help desk coverage if you find the following during your survey:

* Response time is perceived to be too long.

* On average, it takes more than one service call to solve the problem.

* Most problems are software related.

 X-REF Using the techniques described in Chapter 10, will help you lower your costs and increase your service.

Reduce Cost of Information Storage

Paper. That's all that needs to be said. Look around your office at the mounds of information that resides on paper. You photocopy it, file it, take time to find it, recopy it, rekey it, refile it, and still never seem to be able to get the information when you need it. NetMeeting can help you manage this process and reduce the cost of your information storage.

Analyze Your Current Cost of Information Storage

What do you spend each year on storing information? Use a simple matrix, as shown in Figure 14-4, to find out.

Type of Storage	Cost
Paper Files	
Diskettes	
Xerox Copying	
Optical Disks	
Zip Disks	
Slides	
Color Copies	
Syquest Disks	
Administrative	

Figure 14-4 An information storage matrix.

If the number startles you, use the features of NetMeeting to help organize your information. The File Transfer feature and the Whiteboard will replace costly color copies and slides used in presentations. Virtual conferences will replace the need for memos because you'll have the information you need, when you need it.

You will be amazed at the amount of money you'll save by not storing paper. You'll also be able to find and retrieve the information much faster. However, you do need to have some standards to help facilitate this process. The following "Bonus" section shows you how to use Adobe Acrobat along with NetMeeting to maximize your potential.

14

BONUS

Adobe Acrobat as the Common Denominator

Standards are important. Imagine what the world would be like if we didn't have them. The nozzle at the gas pump may or may not fit your car, every VCR would take a different type of tape, and the electric plug would only fit those sockets designed for that particular model. Life would be chaos.

Well, it's the same in the world of information and communication. Without standards, the person with whom you conference may or may not be able to read your files. There are so many software applications that a common denominator is needed and Adobe Systems has provided just that — Acrobat.

Adobe Acrobat is a software product that results in a file format called .PDF (Portable Document Format). In other words, you can save a document from almost any software application as a .PDF file. Usually, if you can print it, you can save it as a .PDF file. In turn, anyone can then open the file and view it, even if they don't have the software that created it. Figure 14-5 shows an example of an Acrobat file.

Combining Acrobat with NetMeeting results in smoother communications. When you use the File Transfer feature, you can save almost anything as a .PDF file and send it to anyone or everyone in the conference. You will be assured that anyone can open and read the file.

 WEB PATH Well, it's not actually as simple as that. You first need to make sure that everyone in your meeting who is receiving your .PDF file has The Adobe Acrobat Reader installed on their systems. Thankfully, it's available as a free download at the Adobe site:

```
http://www.adobe.com
```

Figure 14-5   An Adobe Acrobat file.

To send an Acrobat file using the File Transfer feature, follow these steps:

1. Launch NetMeeting and connect to a ULS server, as described in Chapter 1.

2. Address and connect to a conference participant, as described in Chapter 2.

3. Inform the remote participant(s) that you are going to transfer a .PDF file.

4. Highlight the name of the participant in the Current Call window to send a file to that specific person, or leave all names unselected to send the file to everyone in the conference.

5. Choose Tools → Transfer → Send File , or press Control+F.

6. Using the Windows directory hierarchy, choose a .PDF file to send by using the pop-up menu to navigate to the appropriate file.

7. Click the file you want to send.

8. Click Send. The .PDF file is then sent to the designated participants in the conference.

9. If the file transfer was successful, you will receive notification.

10. Click OK to complete the .PDF file transfer.

Summary

In this chapter, you discovered some of the benefits that come with using NetMeeting in your business. You can lower costs, provide better customer service, increase the level of technical support, and manage information in a better way.

You can use NetMeeting to solve many business problems. Be creative. Experiment with each feature and discover how you can use NetMeeting to make your business and your business life stronger.

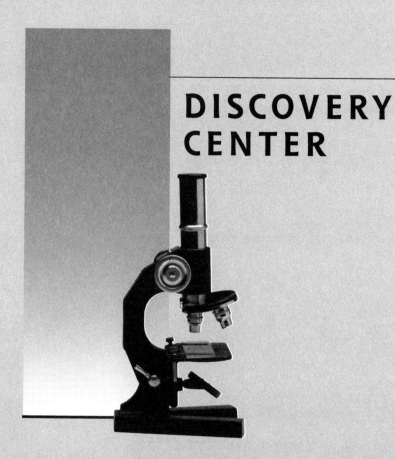

DISCOVERY CENTER

Here you'll find quick, step-by-step synopses of the main skills covered in each chapter.

Chapter 1

How to start NetMeeting   (page 10)

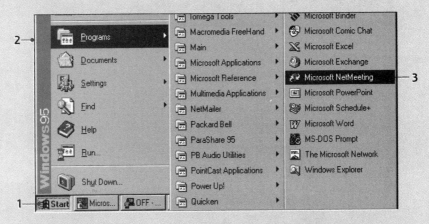

1. Click **Start** .

2. Click **Programs** .

3. Click **Microsoft NetMeeting** .

How to select a menu command   (page 18)

1. Click the menu name to open the menu.

2. Click the appropriate command in the menu.

How to use the main toolbar   (page 22)

Find the main toolbar and click the appropriate button to access the command.

How to set the general preferences   (page 22)

1. Choose **Tools** → **Options** from the main menu.

2. The NetMeeting Options window appears showing the General preferences tab window, pictured as follows.

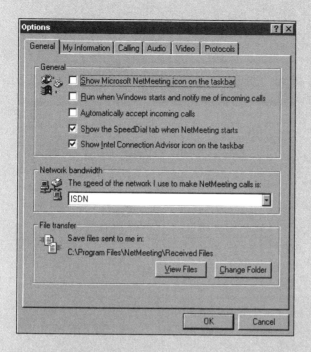

3. Set your preferences by checking the appropriate options.

4. Click OK.

Touring NetMeeting's main features (page 23)

Feature	Function
THE INTERNET PHONE	Talking over the Internet
APPLICATION SHARING	Share a program with one or more users
SHARED CLIPBOARD	Copy and paste information across the country
FILE TRANSFERS	Send files to one or more users
THE WHITEBOARD	Use graphics to communicate your message
CHATTING	A text-based method of speaking in NetMeeting
VIDEO CONFERENCE	Send and receive live video communications
USER LOCATION SERVICE DIRECTORY	The worldwide dynamic phone book

Chapter 2

How to tune your audio   (page 35)

1. Launch NetMeeting by following the steps outlined in Chapter 1.
2. Choose Tools → Audio Tuning Wizard .
3. Click the Next button.
4. Choose the appropriate wave device.
5. Click Next.
6. Click the type of connection you will be using.
7. Click Next.
8. Click the Start Recording button and read the text aloud.
9. Click Next.
10. Click the Finish button.

How to address a phone call   (page 37)

1. Choose Call → New Call from the menu bar, or click the Call icon on the main toolbar.

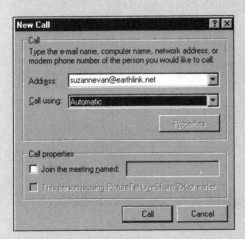

2. In the Address window, type the identity of the computer you are calling.

   Call using will not show up if a modem was not chosen during the installation of NetMeeting. If you chose the Internet as the connection means, Call using will only come up if there is an address problem. Then the Advanced Call dialog box appears, and Call using is one of the options in the Advanced Call dialog box.

3. In the Call using pop-up window, specify whether you are using a modem or a network connection along with the protocol you are using. For now, choose Automatic.

How to place a phone call   (page 38)

1. Complete the steps for addressing a call, and then click Call.

2. An incoming dialog box appears on the computer of the person you are trying to call.

3. Upon acceptance of the call, the Current Call window will list you and the person you called.

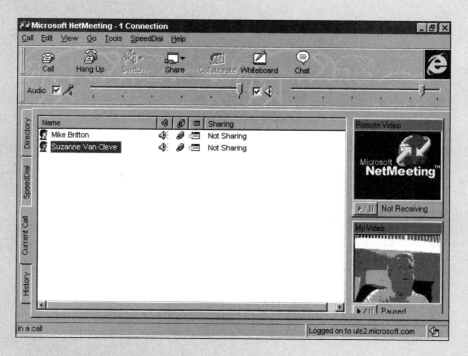

4. Talk into the microphone and listen through the speakers.

5. Notify the participants in the conference that you are hanging up, and then click Hang Up from the main toolbar.

Chapter 3

How to select Application Sharing   (page 48)

Choose │ Tools │ → │ Share Application │ from the menu bar, or click the Share button on the main toolbar. A pop-up menu lists the applications that are available to share.

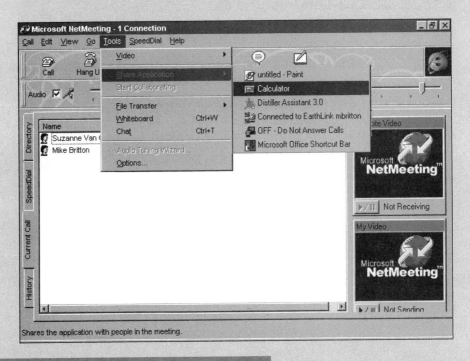

How to share an application   (page 51)

1. Launch NetMeeting and connect to a ULS server.

2. Address and connect to a remote conference participant.

3. Inform the remote participant that you are going to share an application.

4. Choose │ Tools │ → │ Share Application │ from the menu bar, or click the Share button in the main toolbar.

5. Click the application that you want to share and a dialog box appears.

6. Click OK.

7. Click the application in the Windows status bar.

In a call

8. Click Collaborate in the main toolbar.

9. Arrange your desktop space so that you can access other NetMeeting features and controls.

10. Double-click in the Shared Application window to take control of the cursor.

11. Choose `Tools` → `Share Application` from the menu bar.

12. Click the application you want to stop sharing.

13. Inform the participants that the conference is over.

14. Choose `Call` → `Hang Up` from the menu bar, or click the Hang Up button on the main toolbar.

Chapter 4

How to select File Transfer   (page 63)

Choose `Tools` → `File Transfer` → `Send File` from the menu bar.

How to transfer a file   (page 63)

1. Launch NetMeeting and connect to a ULS server, as described in Chapter 1.

2. Address and connect to a conference participant, as described in Chapter 2.

3. Inform the remote participant(s) that you are going to transfer a file.

4. Choose `Tools` → `File Transfer` → `Send File` from the menu bar.

5. Using the Windows directory hierarchy, choose a file to send by using the pop-up menu to navigate to the appropriate file.

6. Click the file you want to send.

7. Click the Send button. The file is sent to all the participants in the conference.

8. If the file transfer was successful, you will receive notification.

9. Click OK to complete the file transfer.

1. Launch NetMeeting and connect to a ULS server, as described in Chapter 1.

2. Address and connect to a conference participant, as described in Chapter 2.

3. A participant informs you that a file is being transferred, and the Virus-Warning dialog appears.

4. Choose one of the three options offered by the Virus-Warning dialog box: Choose Close to close the window and store the file; choose Open to open the folder where the file has been transferred; choose Delete to remove the transferred file from your computer.

Chapter 5

You can select the Whiteboard one of four ways:

* Choose `Tools` → `Whiteboard` from the menu bar.
* Click the Whiteboard icon on the main toolbar.
* Press Control+W.
* Click the NetMeeting icon in the taskbar to bring the application into focus, or to the front; then click the Whiteboard icon.

1. Launch NetMeeting and connect to a ULS server, as described in Chapter 1.

2. Address and connect to a conference participant or participants, as described in Chapter 2.

3. Inform the remote participant(s) that you are going to use the Whiteboard.

4. Press Control+W.

5. Arrange your workspace.

6. Use the drawing feature to communicate your message.

7. Choose **Edit** → **Copy** to copy items to the clipboard.

8. Choose **Edit** → **Paste** to paste items on the clipboard into the Whiteboard document window.

9. Click the Insert New Page button to add additional pages.

10. Click the Remote Pointer icon and the Highlighter to emphasize your message.

Remote pointer

11. Choose `File` → `Save` to save the Whiteboard document created in the conference.

12. Choose `File` → `Exit` to leave the Whiteboard feature.

Chapter 6

How to select Chat (page 106)

You can select Chat one of four ways:

* Choose `Tools` → `Chat` from the menu bar.
* Click the Chat icon on the main toolbar.
* Press Control+T.
* Click the NetMeeting icon in the taskbar, and then click the Chat icon.

How to conduct a Chat session (page 116)

1. Launch NetMeeting and connect to a ULS server, as described in Chapter 1.

2. Address and connect to a conference participant or participants, as described in Chapter 2.

3. Inform the remote participant(s) that you are going to use the Chat feature.

4. Press Control+T.

5. Arrange your workspace for the type of conference you are conducting.

6. Type your message into the Edit window.

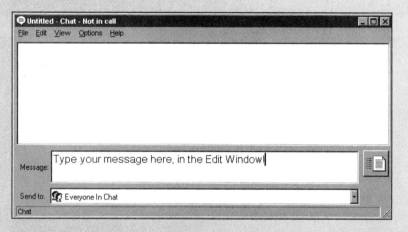

7. Click the Send Message button to the right of the Edit window or press Enter.

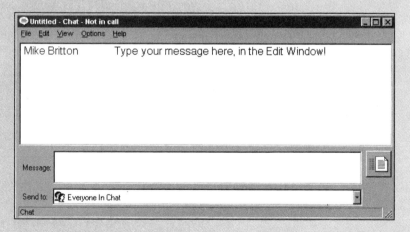

8. Wait for other participants to respond; their reply will appear in the Chat area.

9. Enter a reply in the Edit window and press Enter.

10. Continue the conference until you are ready to end the Chat.

11. Choose `File` → `Save` to save the Chat session document created in the conference.

12. Choose `File` → `Exit` to leave the Chat feature.

Chapter 7

How to set the preferences   (page 126)

1. Display the NetMeeting Options window by choosing `Tools` → `Options` from the menu bar.

2. Click Automatically send video at the start of each call to send video to participants when you launch NetMeeting.

3. Click Automatically receive video at the start of each call to receive video from participants when you launch NetMeeting.

4. Click one of the three image size options. For now, click Medium.

5. Move the Send Quality slider to the left (Low) to increase the video compression. The motion is faster but the image quality is lower.

6. Move the Video Quality slider to the right (High) to decrease the video compression. The motion is slower but the quality is better.

7. Click the Source button to access the camera adjustments dialog box.

8. Adjust the setting for Brightness, Hue, Black Level , and Saturation by moving the sliders, or click Auto Brightness and Auto Hue to have the camera make these adjustments automatically. (See the manual that shipped with your camera for complete instructions.)

9. Click OK in the camera adjustments dialog box.

10. Click OK on the Video tab of the NetMeeting Options window to complete setting the video preferences.

How to select Video Conferencing   (page 130)

1. Choose `Tools` → `Video` → `Send` from the menu bar.

2. Choose `Tools` → `Video` → `Receive` from the menu bar to view the remote participant in a video conference. This option will not be accessible if the remote participant does not have video capabilities.

1. Launch NetMeeting and connect to a ULS server, as described in Chapter 1.

2. Address and connect to a conference participant, as described in Chapter 2.

3. Choose Tools → Video → Send from the menu bar.

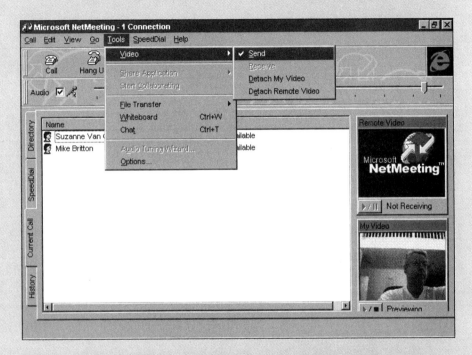

4. Choose Tools → Video → Receive from the menu bar to view the remote participant in a video conference.

5. Conduct your video conference using Audio, Chat, Whiteboard, or any other NetMeeting feature.

6. Click the Hang Up button from the main toolbar to end the conference.

7. Click the Close box in the upper-right corner of the My Video window.

8. Click OK and your video window disappears.

Chapter 8

How to select a ULS   (page 143)

1. Click the Directory pop-up window in the main NetMeeting window.

2. Click the ULS server to which you want to connect. NetMeeting automatically connects you to that directory server.

3. The dynamic ULS directory appears in the Directory window.

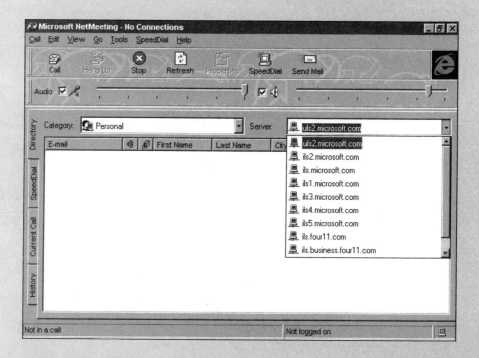

How to update a ULS directory   (page 148)

1. Click the Directory Refresh button located to the left of the ULS Directory pop-up menu.

2. NetMeeting automatically updates the ULS directory to which you are currently connected.

3. Click the Stop Refresh button located to the right of the Directory Refresh button to stop the update.

How to customize a ULS field   (page 149)

1. Move the cursor to the field names in the ULS Directory window.

2. Click and hold one of the dividing lines. The cursor changes to indicate that you can adjust the size of the field.

3. Move the cursor to the right to increase the size of the field, and to the left to decrease the size of the field.

How to sort a ULS field   (page 150)

1. Position the cursor on the name of the field in the ULS Directory window that you want to sort.

2. Click the field name.

3. NetMeeting sorts the field in alphabetical order from A to Z.

4. Click the field name again and the field is sorted from Z to A.

Chapter 9

How to plan a virtual meeting   (page 155)

To plan for a virtual meeting, do the following:

* Decide who will lead the meeting and who will participate.
* Decide which media to use (audio, video, chat).
* Set an agenda.
* Notify participants of the time, place, and agenda.
* Take and distribute minutes.

How to conduct a virtual meeting   (page 159)

1. Get everyone connected.

2. Set the ground rules for the meeting.

3. Introduce the participants.

4. Review the agenda.

5. Use the Audio feature in the meeting.

6. Use the Video feature in the meeting.

7. Share applications during the meeting.

8. Draw on the Whiteboard.

9. Wrap up the meeting.

Chapter 10

How to conduct a virtual customer service call   (page 180)

1. Choose [Call] → [New Call] from the menu bar.

2. In the Address window, type the name of the customer you are calling.

3. Click Call.

4. To answer your call, the customer will click Accept.

5. Talk into the microphone, listen through the speakers, and view the video window.

6. Inform your customer that you are going to share your customer service database.

7. Choose [Tools] → [Share Application] from the menu bar.

8. Click the database and a dialog box appears.

9. Click OK.

10. Click the database in the Windows status bar.

11. Click Collaborate in the main toolbar.

12. Arrange your desktop space so that you can access other NetMeeting features and controls.

13. Double-click in the Shared Application window to take control of the cursor.

14. Enter the appropriate information or have the customer enter the information.

15. When you have completed typing the customer service information, choose `Tools` → `Share Application` from the menu bar.

16. Click the database to stop sharing.

17. Continue the customer service call, accessing other features of NetMeeting or the database as needed.

18. When you have concluded the call, click Hang Up from the main toolbar.

19. You are now ready to make another call or exit the program.

How to conduct a virtual technical support call   (page 183)

1. To answer the call, click Accept.

2. Upon acceptance of the call, the Connection window will list you and the troubled user.

3. Talk into the microphone, listen through the speakers, and view the video window.

4. Try to assess the severity of the problem.

5. Inform the user that you need to take control of their computer.

6. Ask the user to launch Windows Explorer from the `Start` menu.

7. Tell the user to choose `Tools` → `Share Application` from the menu bar in NetMeeting.

8. Ask the user to click Windows Explorer, and a dialog box will appear.

9. Tell the user to click OK.

10. Ask the user to click Windows Explorer in the Windows status bar.

11. Tell the user to click the Collaborate button in the main toolbar.

12. Ask the user to maximize the Windows Explorer window; then tell him or her to sit back and relax while you solve the problem.

13. Arrange your desktop space so that you can access other NetMeeting features and controls.

14. Double-click in the Windows Explorer shared window to take control of the cursor. You now have complete control of the user's computer.

15. Diagnose and fix the problem.

16. When you complete the task, ask the user to choose Tools → Share Application from the menu bar.

17. Tell the user to click Windows Explorer icon, and he or she will stop sharing.

18. When you have concluded the call, click Hang Up from the main toolbar.

19. You are now ready to answer another call or exit the program.

Chapter 11

A desk: Pick one that's the right height for you to work on a computer.

A comfortable ergonomic chair: Get a working-person's chair with a contoured back and cushioned arms if you do a lot of computer work.

Phone lines: You'll need to be separate from your family phone line, and get two additional phone lines if you can: one for voice and one for a computer.

Environment: Remember that you'll spend a lot of time in this room when you're telecommuting. Make your environment professional and pleasant.

Coffee break items: You may want to get a coffee maker and small refrigerator for your office to avoid distractions during the day.

For a home office computer to telecommute, you'll need the following:

Adequate RAM: A minimum of 16MB, 32 preferred.

A big hard drive: Get a 1GB drive, minimum.

Sound and video: Make sure you get a sound card and consider buying a video camera.

A big monitor: Get a 17-inch monitor even though it costs more.

A modem: Get one that's as fast as is available; the latest standard for regular phone lines is 33.6 baud.

A personal scanner: Consider buying a PaperPort or other small desktop scanner for digitizing those odd pieces of paper.

A printer: If you do a lot of printing, or print large graphic files of charts or pictures, spring for a laser printer.

Chapter 12

Distance learning combines the following technologies for effective education:

Discussion groups: Participants can share information by posting questions, answers, and queries about the subject in a common "database" that's accessible online.

Chat groups: These are interactive, with all participants being online at the same time and having a dialog of words on the screen.

Video and audio conferencing: With these tools, you can see and hear multiple participants in the session, just like being in the same classroom.

Whiteboard: "Show" ideas with the Whiteboard feature, whether you show freeform sketches or detailed diagrams.

E-mail: Participants can one-on-one e-mail other students, exchanging notes, ideas, and so on.

Online resources: Participants can have virtually instantaneous access to a wealth of online information, including a log of homework assignments, reference works, and resources.

If you're leading an online course, be sure to do the following:

Establish the subject. Clearly define the goals and scope of the course.

Establish the audience. Define who the course is appropriate for.

Establish the communication method. Decide which of the online tools will work best for your subject matter: chat groups, discussion groups, e-mail, or other online forums.

Establish the time frame. Clarify how much time participants will have to spend, both online and offline, to achieve the goals of the course.

Prepare the course. Create an outline and define modules for your course.

Promote the session. Let people know about your online course.

Chapter 13

How to find a friend   (page 206)

1. Click the Directory tab in the main NetMeeting window.

2. Click the ULS server to which you want to connect.

3. Position the cursor on the Last Name field in the ULS Directory window.

4. Click.

5. NetMeeting sorts the field in alphabetical order from A to Z.

6. Scroll through the list to find a friend to call.

7. Follow the instructions in Chapter 2 to place the call.

Guidelines for personal use (page 215)

Follow these guidelines when you use NetMeeting for personal use:

* Be cautious when you enter personal information; there are wicked people out there that want to take advantage of you.

* Carefully consider not contacting someone that displays an X-rated message in the Comment section. The Comment field gives you a glimpse of the person's personality.

* Never give out your home address or any other personal information over the Internet.

* Never configure NetMeeting to automatically answer with the video feature. You may not be ready to be in pictures.

* When you do find that special someone on NetMeeting, list both on the same ULS server. It will simplify the connection process.

Chapter 14

Use NetMeeting to lower travel costs if   (page 222)

* One person travels to a remote location to visit one person.
* Groups of people travel to the same location for a meeting.
* The purpose of the travel is to share a presentation or information.
* The travel happens on a regular schedule.

Use NetMeeting to improve information access if   (page 224)

* You have four or more meetings per day.
* You reply to the same e-mail more than once.
* You leave more than three voice-mail messages per day.

How to use NetMeeting with Acrobat   (page 229)

1. Launch NetMeeting and connect to a ULS server, as described in Chapter 1.

2. Address and connect to a conference participant, as described in Chapter 2.

3. Inform the remote participant(s) that you are going to transfer a .PDF file.

4. Choose `Tools` → `File Transfer` → `Send File` from the menu bar.

5. Using the Windows directory hierarchy, choose a .PDF file to send by using the pop-up menu to navigate to the appropriate file.

6. Click the file you want to send.

7. Click Send. The .PDF file is sent to all the participants in the conference.

8. If the file transfer was successful, you will receive notification.

9. Click OK to complete the .PDF file transfer.

VISUAL INDEX

Getting Started with NetMeeting

How to start NetMeeting (page 10)

How to configure NetMeeting (pages 12, 22)

How to place a call (page 37)

How to use the tab windows (pages 15–18)

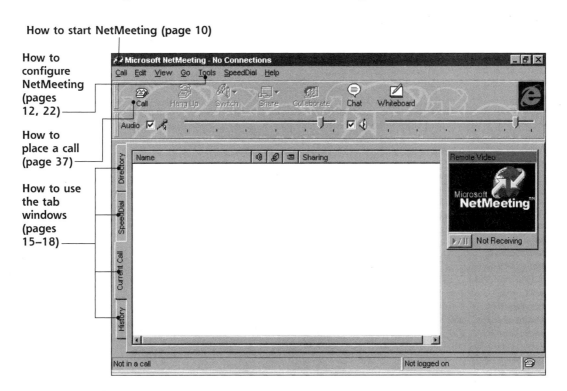

Telephoning on the Internet

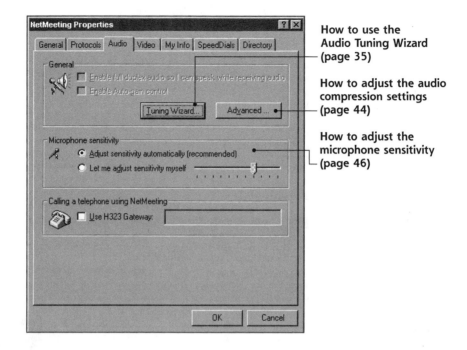

How to use the
Audio Tuning Wizard
(page 35)

How to adjust the audio
compression settings
(page 44)

How to adjust the
microphone sensitivity
(page 46)

Sharing Applications

How to select
the Application
Sharing feature
(page 48)

How to protect
yourself from
the dangers
of sharing
applications
(page 49)

How to
decide what
applications
to share
(page 52)

Transferring Files

How to select
File Transfer
preferences
(page 60)

How to send
files to more
than one
participant
(page 63)

How to open
received files
(page 65)

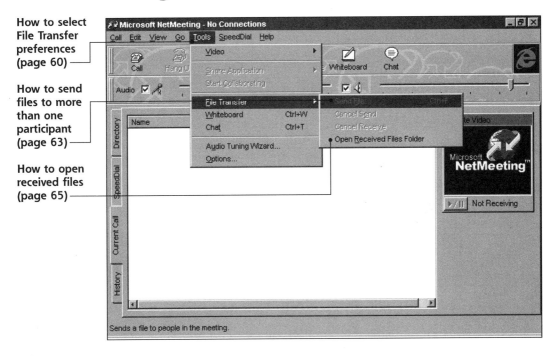

The Whiteboard: A Virtual Blackboard

How to
select the
Whiteboard
(page 72)

How to use
the tools
(pages
82–84)

How to
navigate the
Whiteboard
(page 85)

How to work
with text
(pages 78, 86)

How to select
custom colors
(page 74)

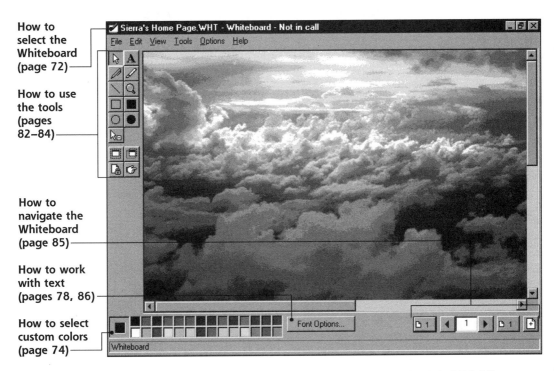

Chatting Away on the Net

How to
select Chat
(page 106)

How to
set Chat
preferences
(page 107)

How to
use the
Chat feature
(page 116)

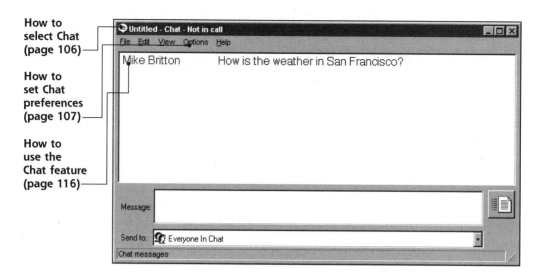

Video Conferencing with NetMeeting

How to
activate the
video feature
(page 130)

How to select a
video camera
(page 124)

How to
prepare your
environment
for a video
conference
(pages
125–126)

How to copy
and zoom the
video window
(page 133)

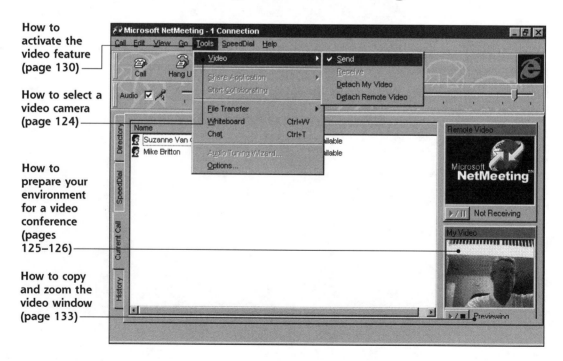

Using the ULS

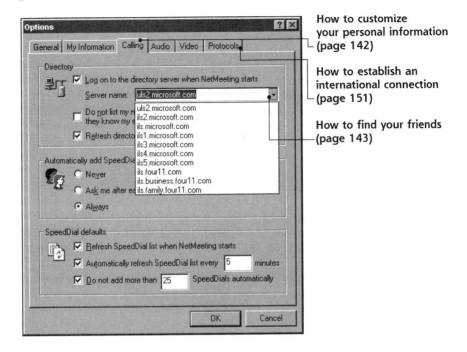

How to customize
your personal information
(page 142)

How to establish an
international connection
(page 151)

How to find your friends
(page 143)

Collaborating on the Net

How to
choose the
Whiteboard
feature
(page 72)

How to keep
everyone
happy in
a virtual
meeting
(page 158)

How to
conduct
a virtual
meeting
(page 159)

How to
change pages
with the
Whiteboard
(page 85)

GETTING MICROSOFT NETMEETING

There are two ways you can get your copy of Microsoft NetMeeting. You can install it from the CD-ROM included with this book or you can download it directly from the Microsoft Web site. The first method is probably the easiest; the second method is useful to know in case you want to upgrade to a later version of NetMeeting sometime in the future. (The current version is 2.0.)

In addition, you can find NetMeeting bundled with some conferencing applications and software packages.

To install NetMeeting from the CD, follow these steps:

1. Insert the CD into the CD-ROM drive. The Internet Explorer setup program will automatically start. If it doesn't, select **Start** → **Run**, type **d:\setup.exe**, and click OK.

2. On the installer main screen, click the appropriate installation option for your operating system (Windows 95 or NT) and follow the on-screen instructions.

3. In the dialog box that appears, click OK to confirm that you want to install NetMeeting.

4. Read the Microsoft End-User License Agreement. If you agree to the terms, click Yes; if you do not agree to the terms of the agreement, click No and discontinue the installation.

5. After a few seconds, you'll be prompted to specify where on your hard drive to install NetMeeting. By default, NetMeeting will be installed in the C:\Program Files\NetMeeting directory. If you'd like it installed to another directory, enter the full pathname of the directory you want. Click OK to begin installation.

To download NetMeeting from the Microsoft Web site, follow these steps:

1. Connect to your Internet Service Provider and launch your browser.

2. Go to http://www.microsoft.com/ie/download/.

3. Scroll to the area on the screen where Microsoft NetMeeting is discussed and click on the Download button.

4. Select the version of NetMeeting that you want to download from the drop-down list, then click on the Next button.

5. Choose the appropriate language (probably U.S. English for you) and click on the Next button.

6. Select a download site from the list provided and click on the .exe file link to start the download procedure. Generally, you want to select a geographic location close to your own. It takes approximately 20 minutes at 28.8 bps to download NetMeeting.

APPENDIX B

SYSTEM REQUIREMENTS AND CONFIGURATION

System Requirements

To be able to run NetMeeting, you must have the following system requirements:

* 486/66 or higher processor (Pentium is recommended)
* Minimum 8MB of RAM (16MB is recommended)
* Microsoft Windows 95
* LAN connection, ISDN connection, or 14.4 Kbps or higher modem connection (28.8 Kbps is recommended)
* Sound card, speakers, and microphone (to use the audio features)
* Video camera (to use the video features)

Full and Half Duplex

NetMeeting supports both full- and half-duplex sound cards. If you are using a half-duplex card, you cannot talk into the microphone and listen to the speakers at the same time. If you are using a full-duplex card, you can both talk and listen at the same time. During the initial installation of NetMeeting, the Wizard conducts a detection process to determine whether you have a full- or half-duplex card. If you change your sound card after the installation of NetMeeting, or if you are having trouble with your sound card, you can always do a manual check to see if it is operating properly. To do a manual check, see the next section.

To determine if you have full or half duplex, follow these steps:

1. Click Start.

2. Click Programs .

3. Click Accessories .

4. Click Multimedia .

5. Click Sound Recorder .

6. Repeat the first five steps to launch a second Sound Recorder.

7. On the first Sound Recorder, play a .WAV file that is at least 30 seconds long.

8. While the .WAV file is playing on the first Sound Recorder, record a .WAV file on the second Sound Recorder.

If you can record a .WAV file on the second Sound Recorder while the first Sound Recorder plays a .WAV file, you have a full-duplex sound card. If you are unable to record the .WAV file, you have a half-duplex sound card.

NOTE The sound card drivers shipped with Windows 95 do not support full-duplex audio. If your sound card supports full duplex, you must obtain drivers that support full duplex.

Connections

etMeeting can establish a connection over a LAN, the Internet using a standard phone line, or an ISDN line. If you establish the connection over a LAN, the TCP/IP or IPX/SPX protocol must be used. If you establish a connection over the Internet, the TCP/IP protocol must be used.

To configure NetMeeting for a particular connection, follow these steps:

1. Click Tools → Options .

2. Click the Protocol tab.

3. Click the TCP/IP check box if you want to use this protocol.

4. Click the Network (IPX) check box to establish a LAN connection.

5. Click the Modem check box to establish a connection over a phone line.

You can configure NetMeeting to establish a connection with other conferencing programs. NetMeeting is based on the ActiveX Conferencing platform, and it conforms to the International Telecommunications Union (ITU) T.120

conferencing specification. Therefore, NetMeeting is compatible with any other conferencing program that is based on this standard, including the following:

* ShareVision from Creative Labs
* ProShare Conferencing Video System from Intel
* LiveShare Plus from PictureTel Corporation

For up-to-the-minute information on NetMeeting, visit the Microsoft Web site at the following URL:

```
http://www.microsoft.com/netmeeting
```

APPENDIX C

GETTING MICROSOFT CHAT

There are two ways you can get your copy of Microsoft Chat. You can install it from the CD-ROM included with this book or you can download it directly from the Microsoft Web site. The first method is probably the easiest; the second method is useful to know in case you want to upgrade to a later version of Chat sometime in the future. (The current version is 2.0.)

To install Microsoft Chat from the CD, follow these steps:

1. Insert the CD into the CD-ROM drive. The Internet Explorer setup program will automatically start. If it doesn't, select `Start` → `Run`, type **d:\setup.exe**, and click OK.

2. On the installer main screen, click the option to install Chat on either Windows 95 and NT and follow the on-screen instructions.

3. Click Yes in the dialog box that appears to confirm that you want to install Chat.

4. Read the Microsoft End-User License Agreement. If you agree to the terms, click Yes; if you do not agree to the terms of the agreement, click No and discontinue the installation.

5. After a few seconds, you'll be prompted to specify where on your hard drive to install Chat. By default, Chat will be installed in the C:\Program Files\Chat directory. If you'd like to install it to another directory, enter the full pathname of the directory you want. Click OK to begin the installation.

To download Chat from the Microsoft Web site, follow these steps:

1. Connect to your Internet Service Provider and launch your browser.

2. Go to http://www.microsoft.com/ie/download/.

3. Scroll to the area on the screen where Microsoft Chat is discussed and click on the Download button.

4. Select the version of Chat that you want to download from the drop-down list, then click on the Next button.

5. Choose the appropriate language (probably U.S. English for you) and click on the Next button.

6. Select a download site from the list provided and click on the .exe file link to start the download procedure. Generally, you want to select a geographic location close to your own. It takes approximately 10 minutes at 28.8 bps to download Chat.

Chat Requirements

Microsoft Chat requires the following configuration:

* 486/66 or higher (Pentium is recommended)
* 8MB of RAM or higher (16MB is recommended)
* Windows 95
* 256 color video display
* 9600 bps modem or faster

Chat FAQs

Using Microsoft Chat is easy. But you may find yourself having some questions about how to use it. Below are some common questions people have when getting started with Chat, along with the answers:

Q: How much space will Chat require?

A: Chat is 1.1MB compressed and takes up 4.1MB of space when installed.

Q: Can I create my own characters?

A: At this time, you can only use the characters provided.

Q: Can I create my own environment?

A: At this time, you can only use the backgrounds provided.

Q: How can I tell the identity of duplicate characters?

A: Place the mouse on a character and the user name will appear.

Q: How do I get more panels to fit on the screen?

A: You can maximize the program, increase your screen resolution, or make the member list thinner.

Visit the Microsoft Chat Web site to learn about the latest enhancements that make Chat even more cool, including new downloadable characters and backgrounds, as well as integration with Internet Explorer and NetMeeting. The site is at:

```
http://www.microsoft.com/ie/chat/
```

NETMEETING FAQS

E ven after reading this book, you'll find yourself with questions about using NetMeeting. Don't feel alone. Here is a list of frequently asked questions concerning NetMeeting, along with the answers:

Q: How do I block calls?

A: Choose `Call` → `Do Not Disturb`.

Q: How do I find the e-mail address of a remote caller?

A: Right-click on the name of the remote user.

Q: How do I get to the NetMeeting Web site?

A: Click the NetMeeting Home Page button on the toolbar.

Q: How do I create a SpeedDial to send to remote callers or imbed in my Home Page?

A: Click `Call` → `Create SpeedDial`, and then choose `Save`.

Q: Can I view a ULS server as a Web page?

A: Yes. Type `http://<uls server name>`

Q: Can I add a link on my Web Page to allow people to call via NetMeeting?

A: Yes. Go to the NetMeeting Web site at `http://www.microsoft.com/netmeeting` for current details.

Q: Can I reposition the ULS directory column heads?

A: Yes. Click the column head and drag left or right.

Q: Can more than two people use the audio features of NetMeeting at one time?

A: No. Only two people can use the audio feature at any one time.

Q: How can I tell who is sharing an application?

A: Look in the upper-right corner of the application window; the name of the person sharing the application is displayed.

Q: How can I speed up a conference using the Whiteboard?

A: Have each participant launch the Whiteboard before joining the conference.

Q: Can I save the transcript of a Chat conference?

A: Yes. Choose `File` → `Save` after you finish the Chat session.

Q: Do I need a video camera to receive a video image in NetMeeting?

A: No. You can receive images; however, you need a camera to send.

INDEX

Audio Tuning Wizard, 13, 35–36, 40, 44
    <Back button, 36
    connection type, 36
    Start Recording button, 36

B

BMP files, 168
board meetings, 223
Browse for Folder window, 60
budgets, preparing and presenting, 56–57
business uses for NetMeeting, 221
    better customer service, 225–226
    instant access to people and
        information, 224
    reduced information storage costs, 227
    reducing travel costs, 222–224
    technical support, 226

C

Call using pop-up window, 160
Call→Exit command, 43
Call→New Call command, 37, 160, 180
Camera Adjustments dialog box, 129–130
Chat feature, 28, 105
    adjusting formats, 109–112
    cautions, 114
    conducting chat session, 116–118
    Control+T keyboard command, 106,
        116
    definition of, 113
    displaying messages in single line,
        111–112
    fonts, 107–108
    individual window resizing, 114
    informing participant of Application
        Sharing, 52

message date, 110
message time, 111
participants' names, 110
preferences, 107–112
quitting, 117
saving documents, 117
simultaneous chatting, 114
Smileys and Abbreviations, 114–115
starting, 106
virtual meetings, 163
vs. audio, 114
Whiteboard size, 98
wrapping messages, 112
Chat Format dialog box
    Entire message is on one line option,
        111
    participants' names, 110
    Wrap option, 112
Chat icon, 106
Chat window, 107, 110–111
    adjusting text size, 108
    Internet Phone and, 116
    Video Conference feature and, 116
    Whiteboard and, 116
chatting
    Chat comic strip, 119–122
    conducting session, 116–118
    simultaneous, 114
Circle tool, 87, 90
circles, 90
Clears the current page dialog box, 95
clipboard
    cutting and pasting from Whiteboard,
        93–94
    sharing contents of, 25
Close Video dialog box, 133
Collaborate dialog box, 55
Collaborating dialog box, 51
collaborative artwork, 80
color
    amount of, 76

(continued)

I

IBM Internet Connection, 194
implementing customer service and
    technical support
  cost justification, 177
  going live, 178
  hardware and software needs, 176–177
  installing computers and software, 177
  mapping process, 176
  obtaining approval, 177
  purchasing equipment and software,
    177
  testing, 178
  training, 178
information storage, reduced cost of, 227
infrastructure, 173–174
instant access to people and information,
    224
international connections, 151
international pen pals, 211
Internet
  as worldwide e-mail system, 34
  locating users, 147
  voice calls, 24
Internet Phone feature, 24, 33–42
  addressing voice calls, 37–38
  answering voice calls, 39
  informing participant of Application
    Sharing, 52
  maximizing Chat window, 116
  placing voice calls, 38–40
  Whiteboard size, 98
Internet Telephony, 33–35
intranets
  locating users, 147
  Video Conferencing feature, 131
  voice calls, 24
introducing participants, 161
IP address, 147

IPX/SPX protocol
  audio connection, 44
  voice calls, 38
ISPs (Internet Service Providers), 193–194
  connection information, 11
  selection of, 12
  unsuccessful in connecting to, 12

K

keyboard commands
  Alt+O (Solid Color), 77
  Control+F (Send File), 229
  Control+T (Chat), 106, 116
  Control+W (Whiteboard), 22, 73, 98,
    187, 218
  Control+Z (Undo), 94

L

LAN (local area network) audio
    connection, 44
lighting, 126
Line tool, 87–89
lines, resizing width, 79
LiveShare Plus, 160
locating users, 141, 147
Lotus Organizer, 157

M

main toolbar, 15
  Call button, 37–38, 42, 160–161, 180
  Chat button, 106, 163
  Collaborate button, 51, 55, 165, 181,
    184

programs
    Adobe Acrobat, 68–69, 165–166, 199,
        228–230
    controlling hardware devices, 49
    LiveShare Plus, 160
    Lotus Organizer, 157
    Microsoft Chat, 119–122
    Microsoft Internet Mail, 157
    Microsoft Paint, 80–81
    Microsoft Schedule, 157
    PictureTel LiveShare, 38, 160
    sharing, 25, 47–55, 165–166
    what you can share, 50
proofing documents with File Transfer
       feature and Adobe Acrobat, 68–69

R

Rectangle tool, 87, 89, 100
rectangles, 89
regular meetings, 223
Remote Pointer, 92, 187
research, 217–218
risks in Application Sharing feature,
       49–50
ROI (Return On Investment), 177

S

Save As dialog box, 96
saving
    Chat feature documents, 117
    Whiteboard, 96
scanning documents, 168–170
screen, pasting any area onto
       Whiteboard, 94
Select a File to Send window, 63–64
Select Area icon, 94

Select tool, 86, 94
Select Window icon, 93–94
Send File command, 67, 164
    Control+F keyboard command, 229
setup wizard, 12–14
Shared Application window, 182
Shared Clipboard feature, 25
sharing
    clipboard contents, 25
    folders, 50
    windows, 50
Sharing dialog box, 53
sharing programs, 25, 47–55
    active program window, 54
    bringing application or window to
       front, 53
    cutting or copying text or graphics, 55
    other participants controlling program,
       55
    participant sharing status, 55
    preparing and presenting budgets,
       56–57
    reasons to use, 51–52
    regaining control, 51
    selecting application for, 53
    shared window covered with nonshared
       window, 54
    taking control of cursor, 55
    virtual meetings, 165–166
    what you can share, 50
    working alone or collaborating, 51
Smileys, 114–115
software, maximizing use of, 30–31
Solid Color (Alt+O) keyboard command,
       77
sound card, 13, 35
    enabling full duplex audio, 36–37
SpeedDial tab window, 16–17, 208
Sprynet, 194
Start button, 10

Start menu, 10
Start→Programs command, 159
starting
    Chat feature, 106
    NetMeeting, 10–12
status bar, 18
    conference participants, 39
    hiding/displaying Whiteboard, 74
Stop button, 148
straight lines, 88–89

T

taking minutes in meeting, 158
taskbar
    NetMeeting icon, 73, 106
    Whiteboard button, 73
TCP/IP protocol
    audio connection, 44
    voice calls, 38
technical support, 172–178
    analyzing virtual data, 180
    assessing company needs, 172–174
    capturing virtual data, 179
    conducting, 183–184
    cost justification, 177
    definition of, 171
    establishing goals, 175
    going live, 178
    hardware and software needs, 176–177
    implementing, 175–178
    installing computers and software, 177
    mapping process, 175–176
    obtaining approval, 177
    planning for, 172
    purchasing equipment and software,
        177
    reducing costs of, 226

testing, 178
training, 178
telecommuting
    hardware, 192, 193
    ISPs (Internet Service Providers),
        193–194
    planning for, 191–193
    pros and cons, 189–190
    setting up office, 191–192
    tips, 194–195
text
    adding to Whiteboard, 86–87
    changing font attributes, 87
    editing, 87
    moving, 86
    sharing, 55
Text tool, 86–87, 100, 186
text-based communications, 28
time in messages, 111
time frame, reviewing, 162
title bar, 15
toolbar, 82
    Circle tool, 87, 90
    Draw tool, 87–88
    functionality, 84
    hiding/displaying Whiteboard, 74
    Highlight tool, 91
    Line tool, 79, 87–89
    Lock icon, 80, 99
    Rectangle tool, 87, 89
    Remote Pointer, 92
    Select Area icon, 94
    Select tool, 86, 94
    Select Window icon, 93–94
    Text tool, 78, 86–87
    tools listing, 83
Tools→Audio Tuning Wizard command,
    35
Tools→Audio Wizard command, 40
Tools→Chat command, 106

Tools→File Transfer→Send File command,
  63, 164
Tools→Options command, 22, 37, 44, 46,
  60, 126–127, 142, 213
Tools→Share Application command, 48,
  52, 55, 165, 181–182, 184
Tools→Transfer→Send File command, 229
Tools→Video→Receive command,
  131–132
Tools→Video→Send command, 130–131
Tools→Whiteboard command, 72, 218
transferring files, 26–27, 59–67
  Adobe Acrobat files, 229–230
  to all participants, 63–64
  changing folder to save files in, 60
  definition of, 62
  during virtual meeting, 163–164
  to only one participant, 66–67, 164
  receiving files, 65–66
travel costs
  analyzing current budget, 222
  board meetings, 223
  one-on-one meetings, 223
  presentations, 223
  reductions with NetMeeting, 222–224
  regular meetings, 223

U

ULS (User Location Server), 29, 141
  changing directory, 146
  connecting to, 144–145
  listing your name on, 13
  name of, 12
  selecting, 143
ULS directory pop-up menu, 148
ULS directory window
  Comment section, 212–214, 216
  Country field, 211

removing fields, 150
resizing fields in, 149–150
sorting fields alphabetically, 150
Undo (Ctrl+Z) keyboard command, 94
User Location Service directory, 29, 141,
  147
  customizing, 149–150
  IP address, 147
  preferences, 142–143
  removing fields in directory, 150
  resizing fields in directory, 149–150
  setting directory server information,
    142–143
  sorting fields alphabetically, 150
  updating, 148
users
  accessing, 29
  locating, 141, 147

V

video
  automatically sending or receiving, 127
  communications, 28
  image quality, 128–129
video cameras, 124–126
  adjustments, 129–130
  distances to photograph at, 125–126
  lighting, 126
video conferences, conducting, 131–133
Video Conferencing feature, 28, 123
  automatically receiving video, 127
  automatically sending video, 127
  Chat window and, 116
  conducting video conference, 131–133
  copying video image, 133–135
  distance requirements, 125–126
  hardware requirements, 124–126

(continued)

IDG BOOKS WORLDWIDE, INC.
END-USER LICENSE AGREEMENT

READ THIS. You should carefully read these terms and conditions before opening the software packet(s) included with this book ("Book"). This is a license agreement ("Agreement") between you and IDG Books Worldwide, Inc. ("IDGB"). By opening the accompanying software packet(s), you acknowledge that you have read and accept the following terms and conditions. If you do not agree and do not want to be bound by such terms and conditions, promptly return the Book and the unopened software packet(s) to the place you obtained them for a full refund.

1. **License Grant.** IDGB grants to you (either an individual or entity) a nonexclusive license to use one copy of the enclosed software program(s) (collectively, the "Software") solely for your own personal or business purposes on a single computer (whether a standard computer or a workstation component of a multiuser network). The Software is in use on a computer when it is loaded into temporary memory (RAM) or installed into permanent memory (hard disk, CD-ROM, or other storage device). IDGB reserves all rights not expressly granted herein.

2. **Ownership.** IDGB is the owner of all right, title, and interest, including copyright, in and to the compilation of the Software recorded on the disk(s) or CD-ROM ("Software Media"). Copyright to the individual programs recorded on the Software Media is owned by the author or other authorized copyright owner of each program. Ownership of the Software and all proprietary rights relating thereto remain with IDGB and its licensers.

3. **Restrictions On Use and Transfer.**

   (a) You may only (i) make one copy of the Software for backup or archival purposes, or (ii) transfer the Software to a single hard disk, provided that you keep the original for backup or archival purposes. You may not (i) rent or lease the Software, (ii) copy or reproduce the Software through a LAN or other network system or through any computer subscriber system or bulletin-board system, or (iii) modify, adapt, or create derivative works based on the Software.

   (b) You may not reverse engineer, decompile, or disassemble the Software. You may transfer the Software and user documentation on a permanent basis, provided that the transferee agrees to accept the terms and conditions of this Agreement and you retain no copies. If the Software is an update or has been updated, any transfer must include the most recent update and all prior versions.

4. **Restrictions On Use of Individual Programs.** You must follow the individual requirements and restrictions detailed for each individual program in the appendixes of this Book. These limitations are also contained in the individual license agreements recorded on the Software Media. These limitations may include a requirement that after using the program for a specified period of time, the user must pay a registration fee or discontinue use. By opening the Software packet(s), you will be agreeing to abide by the licenses and restrictions for these individual programs that are detailed in the appendixes and on the Software Media. None of the material on this Software Media or listed in this Book may ever be redistributed, in original or modified form, for commercial purposes.

5. Limited Warranty.

(a) IDGB warrants that the Software and Software Media are free from defects in materials and workmanship under normal use for a period of sixty (60) days from the date of purchase of this Book. If IDGB receives notification within the warranty period of defects in materials or workmanship, IDGB will replace the defective Software Media.

(b) IDGB AND THE AUTHORS OF THE BOOK DISCLAIM ALL OTHER WARRANTIES, EXPRESS OR IMPLIED, INCLUDING WITHOUT LIMITATION IMPLIED WARRANTIES OF MERCHANTABILITY AND FITNESS FOR A PARTICULAR PURPOSE, WITH RESPECT TO THE SOFTWARE, THE PROGRAMS, THE SOURCE CODE CONTAINED THEREIN, AND/OR THE TECHNIQUES DESCRIBED IN THIS BOOK. IDGB DOES NOT WARRANT THAT THE FUNCTIONS CONTAINED IN THE SOFTWARE WILL MEET YOUR REQUIREMENTS OR THAT THE OPERATION OF THE SOFTWARE WILL BE ERROR FREE.

(c) This limited warranty gives you specific legal rights, and you may have other rights that vary from jurisdiction to jurisdiction.

6. Remedies.

(a) IDGB's entire liability and your exclusive remedy for defects in materials and workmanship shall be limited to replacement of the Software Media, which may be returned to IDGB with a copy of your receipt at the following address: Software Media Fulfillment Department, Attn.: *Discover Desktop Conferencing with NetMeeting 2.0*, IDG Books Worldwide, Inc., 7260 Shadeland Station, Ste. 100, Indianapolis, IN 46256, or call 1-800-762-2974. Please allow three to four weeks for delivery. This Limited Warranty is void if failure of the Software Media has resulted from accident, abuse, or misapplication. Any replacement Software Media will be warranted for the remainder of the original warranty period or thirty (30) days, whichever is longer.

(b) In no event shall IDGB or the authors be liable for any damages whatsoever (including without limitation damages for loss of business profits, business interruption, loss of business information, or any other pecuniary loss) arising from the use of or inability to use the Book or the Software, even if IDGB has been advised of the possibility of such damages.

(c) Because some jurisdictions do not allow the exclusion or limitation of liability for consequential or incidental damages, the above limitation or exclusion may not apply to you.

7. U.S. Government Restricted Rights.
Use, duplication, or disclosure of the Software by the U.S. Government is subject to restrictions stated in paragraph (c)(1)(ii) of the Rights in Technical Data and Computer Software clause of DFARS 252.227-7013, and in subparagraphs (a) through (d) of the Commercial Computer@mdRestricted Rights clause at FAR 52.227-19, and in similar clauses in the NASA FAR supplement, when applicable.

8. General.
This Agreement constitutes the entire understanding of the parties and revokes and supersedes all prior agreements, oral or written, between them and may not be modified or amended except in a writing signed by both parties hereto that specifically refers to this Agreement. This Agreement shall take precedence over any other documents that may be in conflict herewith. If any one or more provisions contained in this Agreement are held by any court or tribunal to be invalid, illegal, or otherwise unenforceable, each and every other provision shall remain in full force and effect.

CD-ROM Installation Instructions

The CD-ROM contains three programs that you can install: Microsoft Internet Explorer 3.02, Microsoft NetMeeting 2.0, and Microsoft Chat 2.0.

To install Microsoft Internet Explorer:

1. Insert the CD into the CD-ROM drive. The Internet Explorer setup program will automatically start. If it doesn't, select `Start` → `Run`, type **d:\setup.exe**, and click OK.

2. On the installer main screen, click the Internet Connection Wizard option and follow the on-screen instructions.

If you are running Windows NT, the above procedure will not work. Instead, use Windows Explorer to run the file called Ie3inst.exe in the D:\Win95_NT\Eng directory. You run the file by double-clicking it.

To install Microsoft NetMeeting:

1. Run Setup.exe as explained above.

2. Click the appropriate installation option for your operating system (Windows 95 or NT) and follow the on-screen instructions.

3. In the dialog box that appears, click OK to confirm that you want to install NetMeeting.

4. Read the Microsoft End-User License Agreement. If you agree to the terms, click Yes; if you do not agree to the terms of the agreement, click No and discontinue the installation.

5. After a few seconds, you'll be prompted to specify where on your hard drive to install NetMeeting. By default, NetMeeting will be installed in the C:\Program Files\NetMeeting directory. If you'd like it installed to another directory, enter the full pathname of the directory you want. Click OK to begin the installation.

To install Microsoft Chat:

1. Run Setup.exe as explained above.

2. Click the option to install Chat on either Windows 95 and NT and follow the on-screen instructions.

3. Click Yes in the dialog box that appears to confirm that you want to install Chat.

4. Read the Microsoft End-User License Agreement. If you agree to the terms, click Yes; if you do not agree to the terms of the agreement, click No and discontinue the installation.

5. After a few seconds, you'll be prompted to specify where on your hard drive to install Chat. By default, Chat will be installed in the C:\Program Files\Chat directory. If you'd like it installed to another directory, enter the full pathname of the directory you want. Click OK to begin the installation.

When the installation of either of these programs is complete, restart your computer — either by clicking Yes in the dialog box or by clicking No and restarting your computer yourself at another time.

NOTE After installing the various components of Internet Explorer, you may launch the browser by clicking the last link on the installer main screen or by selecting `Start` → `Programs` → `Internet Explorer`. If you are running Windows NT, the link on the installer main screen won't work; you have to launch the browser via the Start menu.

IDG BOOKS WORLDWIDE REGISTRATION CARD

Visit our Web site at http://www.idgbooks.com

ISBN Number: 076458-037X

Title of this book: Discover Desktop Conferencing with NetMeeting™ 2.0

My overall rating of this book: ❏ Very good [1] ❏ Good [2] ❏ Satisfactory [3] ❏ Fair [4] ❏ Poor [5]

How I first heard about this book:

❏ Found in bookstore; name: [6]   ❏ Book review: [7]

❏ Advertisement: [8]   ❏ Catalog: [9]

❏ Word of mouth; heard about book from friend, co-worker, etc.: [10]   ❏ Other: [11]

What I liked most about this book:

What I would change, add, delete, etc., in future editions of this book:

Other comments:

Number of computer books I purchase in a year: ❏ 1 [12] ❏ 2-5 [13] ❏ 6-10 [14] ❏ More than 10 [15]

I would characterize my computer skills as: ❏ Beginner [16] ❏ Intermediate [17] ❏ Advanced [18] ❏ Professional [19]

I use ❏ DOS [20] ❏ Windows [21] ❏ OS/2 [22] ❏ Unix [23] ❏ Macintosh [24] ❏ Other: [25]_____

(please specify)

I would be interested in new books on the following subjects:

(please check all that apply, and use the spaces provided to identify specific software)

❏ Word processing: [26]   ❏ Spreadsheets: [27]

❏ Data bases: [28]   ❏ Desktop publishing: [29]

❏ File Utilities: [30]   ❏ Money management: [31]

❏ Networking: [32]   ❏ Programming languages: [33]

❏ Other: [34]

I use a PC at (please check all that apply): ❏ home [35] ❏ work [36] ❏ school [37] ❏ other: [38] _____

The disks I prefer to use are ❏ 5.25 [39] ❏ 3.5 [40] ❏ other: [41]_____

I have a CD ROM: ❏ yes [42] ❏ no [43]

I plan to buy or upgrade computer hardware this year: ❏ yes [44] ❏ no [45]

I plan to buy or upgrade computer software this year: ❏ yes [46] ❏ no [47]

Name: Business title: [48]   Type of Business: [49]

Address (❏ home [50] ❏ work [51] /Company name:)

Street/Suite#

City [52] /State [53] /Zip code [54]:   Country [55]

❏ **I liked this book!** You may quote me by name in future IDG Books Worldwide promotional materials.

My daytime phone number is _____

IDG BOOKS
WORLDWIDE

THE WORLD OF COMPUTER KNOWLEDGE®

❑ YES!

Please keep me informed about IDG Books Worldwide's
World of Computer Knowledge. Send me your latest catalog.